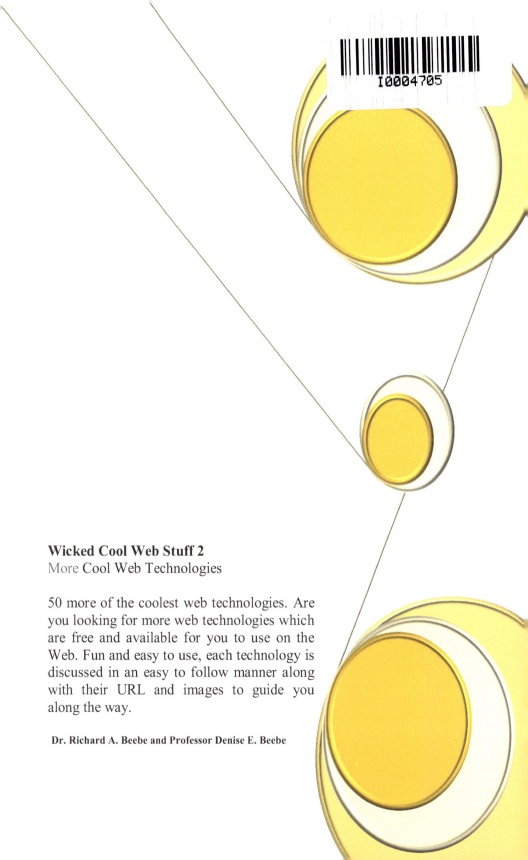

I0004705

Wicked Cool Web Stuff 2
More Cool Web Technologies

50 more of the coolest web technologies. Are
you looking for more web technologies which
are free and available for you to use on the
Web. Fun and easy to use, each technology is
discussed in an easy to follow manner along
with their URL and images to guide you
along the way.

Dr. Richard A. Beebe and Professor Denise E. Beebe

Preface

This is our second book covering web technologies. The reason we created this book is the same reason we created our first book. We created the book to fill a gap that exist between knowing what Web tools are available and knowing how to use them. We hope this book, like our first book, will help you the reader in discovering what is available on the Web and pursue the use of those tools. Everyone should be looking at the cool things available on the web. It is our hope that everyone will look at this book and learn to have fun and make use of these tools.

Why did we write this book? Our reasons have not changed since the writing of our first book. We are teachers –

 We wanted to use technologies which were new on the horizons. We wanted to help students discover new ideas.
We wanted to share what we had found with fellow teachers.
We wanted to let our friends and family know about what is new and exciting on the Web.
We wanted to share the fun.
These were the reasons we wrote this book.

This is a book that can augment any classroom curriculum, no matter what the discipline. Instructors as well as students can examine what is available on the Web. Assignments could be given to examine and use the Web applications in the book. We have used all these tools in the classroom and have found them invaluable.

Education is only one aspect. This book can be used by anyone who wants to take a look at what the Web has to offer. All the tools we look at in the book are free. We hope you will use the book, share it with your friends and have as much fun with the Web applications in the book as we have had.

So open the book and start learning about some "more" Wicked Cool Web Stuff!

Again, we would like to thank all our students, friends and colleagues who without them this book would not be possible. Special thanks to our daughter Jessie who told us to write this second book to share what we have discovered.

Introduction

We have found that the use of web technologies is a great way to engage our students both in and out of the classroom. We have found that with the web technologies and a little imagination we could enhance their learning and our teaching. There are Web applications for just about everything; you can make a cartoon or a comic strip, what a great alternative way to communicate. You can create a voice based, video based, photo based on-line discussion board, what a great way to share ideas. We have found different ways to create presentations, ways to edit photos and text, and so many different tools to aid you. The things we have found are amazing. Some of them are simple little things like creating reversed text, by the way what an interesting way to sign your e-mails. Some of them were just out and out amazing such as a programming language to create an animated comic strip. It's even more amazing when we find it only takes a few minutes to master these tools and they are free to use.

After finding so many Web applications to use we decided to create a second book help to promote and describe 50 more wicked cool web applications/technologies. The new applications we have found are just as fun and engaging as those in our first book.

So after looking and searching we have written "Wicked Cool Web Stuff 2" so that again we can share what we have found and the fun of discovery. These applications are interesting to use, could be used in a classroom with a little creativity, and most importantly are free. We didn't want to write a lot of words about the tools we found; instead we wanted to show the tools. So the following pages contain screenshots with brief explanations of how to use the tool being shown. They are not tutorials, just a brief introduction to get you started. We have tried to include screen shots where we could to give you the reader a better idea of what you will be seeing if you visit these Web sites. We truly hope you will get as much enjoyment from this book as we have gotten in writing it.

So Enjoy....

Richard and Denise Beebe
September, 2011

Table of Contents

Chapter 1 – Photo and Paint

There are many times when we have a photograph that we want to add some content to, or maybe enhance the photo so it looks better. Maybe we don't have a photo to start with, but still want to be able to create our own artistic work of art. In this category we have included just those types of applications.

- Sumo Paint and Aviary let you upload a photo either from your computer or directly from a web site. Once the photo is uploaded you can edit, rotate and even change the look of how it was created.

- Psykopaint will let you actually paint a picture from scratch or paint an existing photo

- PhotoTricks will let your photo become part of a magazine cover.

- Dear Photograph lets you merge old photos with new photos and add comments

- Sketch Artist lets you create your character's face by choosing facial features.

- Shape Collage takes pictures and lets you create shapes with them.

- 3D Package lets you create a 3-D image of a book or a cube.

- PicResize is a great tool for resizing pictures.

All of these have their use and place in and out of education. Experiment with them; we think you will discover that they are really great aids to making education more fun for our students and more fun for us as teachers. Even if you are not an educator these applications will just be Wicked Cool.

1. Sumo Paint

While image editing apps like Photoshop Express or Picnik offer almost everything to edit your photographs online, a limitation with these tools is that you cannot use them to create new images from scratch. That's where

Sumo Paint enters the web application arena. Take a look at Sumo Paint at **http://sumopaint.com**. It should look like Figure 1.1. We love the picture on the beginning screen.

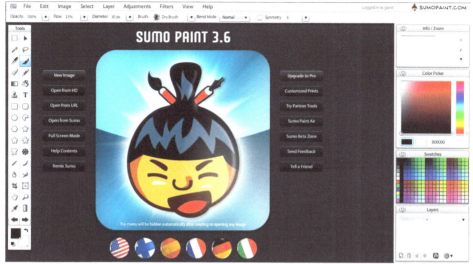

Figure 1.1

This is a pretty complete on-line photo editing package. The tools are very similar to those you find in Photoshop. See Figure 1.2.

The tools are pretty inclusive. You have all your standard tools such as those to rotate and flip the image. There are tools to select parts of the image all the way down to the pixel level. All your typical copy, cut and paste options are available as well as undo and redo. There is also a good assortment of filters available. When you are done you can save your document to your computer in one of three different formats; jpg, png or sumo.

Figure 1.2

On the right side you can find Info/Zoom, Color Picker, Swatches and Layers panels; see Figure 1.3.

Figure 1.3

If you are looking for a Photoshop look alike that is free to use and online than Sumo Paint would be our choice.

Considering it's free, totally on-line, and you can create new images from scratch, this is Wicked Cool.

2. Aviary

Want an easy way to edit your photos? Take a look at Aviary at **http://www.aviary.com/** a free online photo editor. There are a lot of photo editors on the web, but this one is definitely one of the easiest to use. See Figure 1.4.

Figure 1.4

You start by uploading your picture or typing in a URL of where your picture is located on the Web. If you use the URL method it has to be the actual URL of the picture not the URL of the Web page the picture is on. Figure 1.5 shows the picture we uploaded.

Figure 1.5

All the tools that you have available are on the right side of the screen. By clicking on a tool it will take you to that feature. If you click on the Rotate tool it will take you to the Rotate option as can be seen in Figure 1.6.

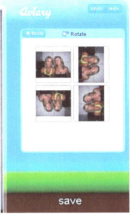

Figure 1.6

You can return back to the tools by clicking on the Tools back button. There are a sufficient number of tools available. You can sharpen the image via a slide bar under the sharpen option. You can whiten, rotate, flip, resize and crop the image by simply clicking on the option available. There are even options to remove redeye and blemishes. All the tools for dealing with color are also available such as Colors, saturation, blur, contrast and brightness. There is a text tool; a drawing tool and even a tool that lets you add stickers to your photo.

We added some text and a sticker that says Happy Father's Day.

Figure 1.7

There are also four tools which will let you change how the photo appears to be taken. Toy camera is pretty cool; it makes it look like it was taken with a low resolution camera. We like Old Photo ourselves, Figure 1.8.

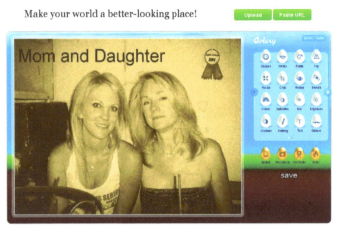

Figure 1.8

We should mention that there is an undo and redo should you select an option that you decide you do not like. The Save option, as seen in Figure 1.9, will let you do several things. You can download it to your machine and save it as a .png file or you can share it on the web.

Figure 1.9

Here it is when we downloaded it.

3.8

Figure 1.10

This is a really easy to use photo editor. Really Wicked Cool.

3. Psykopaint

Figure 1.11

Have you ever wanted to paint? At one time we all have tried our luck at painting only to find out that it's just something that we are not real good at. Psykopaint at **http://www.psykopaint.com** changes all that. The basic idea is really simple, but the results are fantastic. You will need the latest version of Flash for this to work properly, but it will check for you and if you don't have it, it will prompt you to install it. Once installed you are ready to begin. See Figure 1.12.

Figure 1.12

You are first prompted with what you want to paint. You can start from scratch by selecting "Good Old Painting"; or "Try a Sample". We would suggest the "Try a Sample" for the first time out. Basically you don't need to upload your own photo, you can select from several samples as seen in Figure 1.13.

Figure 1.13

We selected the motorcycle.

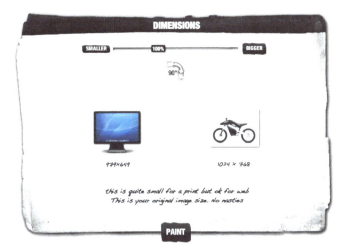

Figure 1.14

It will let you increase the size so it is easier to work on – the size showing in Figure 1.14 is ok for the web but maybe a little small to make a print. We kept the default and pressed the "Paint" button to get started.

Figure 1.15

So this is what it looks like, see Figure 1.15 – with paint brush in hand you are ready to begin. The menu at the bottom of the screen is very easy to follow. The great thing about this is it does most of the work for you. There are four options. Under the File option, Figure 1.16, you will find your menu items related to saving and printing your painting.

Figure 1.16

Notice you can save your finished painting to your computer – yea.

With the brushes option you can select from several different brushes as seen in Figure 1.17.

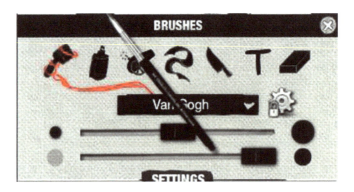

Figure 1.17

If you want you can also create a custom brush by selecting the "Settings" option.

You can change the color with the color option, but as you paint, it will automatically try and select the correct color for you – what a life saver that is.

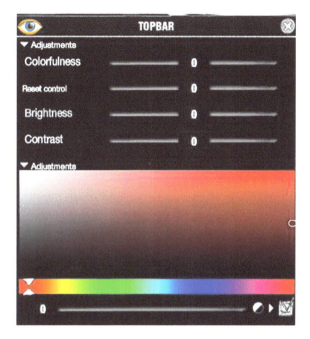

Figure 1.18

The last one "Layers" you don't have access to unless you register the software. (Basically you have to get a paid version to get to this feature.)

On the right side, as shown in Figure 1.19, you will find the slide bars that allow you to change the size of the painting and the opacity, along with the undo and redo buttons.

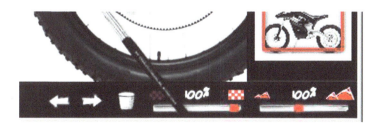

Figure 1.19

The trashcan will let you clear the painting of the current layer. That's about it for tools.

We selected the "Crazy Cannon" as our paintbrush and began painting.

Figure 1.20

Figure 1.20 shows our smoking tires. That's all there is to it. Select your brush and begin painting. We added some text and saved it to our computer.

The neat thing is you can upload your own picture and have all the same capabilities. What a great application. This is Wicked Cool.

.

Figure 1.21

4. Photo Tricks

Figure 1.22

Upload a photo or find one on the web and then use a template to change it. Take a look at **http://www.fototrix.com**.
Start by selecting browse to find a photo, after you find one upload it.
Figure 1.23 shows the photo we uploaded.

Figure 1.23

Next choose a tool for your photo –as can be seen in Figure 1.24, there are a lot of them to select from.

Figure 1.24

We selected "Fake Magazine Cover".

Here you can personalize magazine covers online (no software applications to install, just use your web browser) by uploading digital photos you have on your computer. You can put your face on the cover of many well known magazines (from celebrity gossip zines to children's learning magazines). Simply upload a photograph from your desktop computer or straight from your digital camera (connected to your PC) or use graphics your have collected from the internet! Make your girlfriend a cover girl or make your boyfriend the hunk shown on the front of muscle mags. So many possibilities, even many fake parody magazine designs (they do not really exist) added for fun. Images are free to use in presentations, web pages, ebooks, emails, Word documents, etc. Choose from parody magazine and tabloid covers like Vogue, Discover, GQ, Popular Science, COSMO, ESPN, Esquire, National Geographic, TIME, 17 (teen news), fashion mags, and hundreds more (just do a search)! There are currently **864 magazine templates** (some are better than others, we get some templates donated, more coming soon) for you to mashup your photographs with!

NEW Use your **webcam** to capture the perfect image for your magazine cover HERE (lower quality results, but fun). It's a blast using a digital web camera as you can change facial expressions live to suit the scenes!

Figure 1.25

You can than select the magazine, as seen in Figure 1.26, there are a lot of them to select from.

STEP #2: Choose A Magazine Template

Magazine Template
Page: 1 2 3 4 5 6 7 8 9 10 11 12 13 14 15 16 17 18 19 20

21 22 23 24 25 26 27 28 29 30 31 32 33 34 35 36 37 38 39 40

41 42 43 44

bowling

boxing2

scientific amer

boxing

walking

science enginee   the independent   geo russian   lazy1   walking2

Figure 1.26

We looked through a few and selected "Sexy Girl".

Figure 1.27

To save the image as a jpeg, just right click and select "save picture as" it's that easy.

What you have available to manipulate your photo will be determined by the tool you select. This is really fun to play with. Wicked Cool!

5. DearPhotograph

This is such a simple idea. What a really great idea. Take a look at **http://dearphotograph.com**. As stated on their web site "take a picture of a picture from the past in the present." So basically hold up a picture from the past and match it with the present, then add your caption. Figure 1.28 from their web site shows a dog from the past sitting at the bottom of the stairs. What a great way to add to your memories.

Dear Photograph,
Please tell Tobby I love him. I'm so sorry I didn't have the courage
to say "goodbye".
Always in my heart, Michelle

Figure 1.28

We said it was a simple idea, but why not use it in the classroom. What would your class look like in a school room from the past? What would it be like to have that photo of your students sitting in front of that one room school house? I am sure there are many things that come to mind. At first we could only think of a few, but then all of a sudden we were making lists of ideas. Have you ever had a son or daughter of a previous student in your classroom? There are so many ideas, all of them could be so much fun.

Dear Photograph,
Those were the days, when Mom would put us in matching clothes.
Fabio

Figure 1.29

What a Wicked Cool web site.

6. Sketch Artist

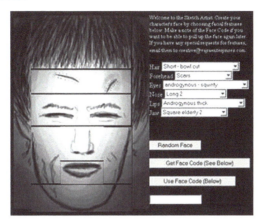

Figure 1.30

Welcome to the Sketch Artist. As seen in Figure 1.30, simply create your character's face by choosing facial features. Make a note of the Face Code if you want to be able to pull up the face again later. Sketch Artist at **http://www.fatesworsethandeath.com/!FWTD/sketchartist/FWTDsketchartist.htm** is a pretty cool application. By selecting different hair, forehead, eyes, nose, lips and jaw you can create a sketch of someone from memory or just create a funny sketch of a person. You can even pick a random face to begin with. Here we picked a few options to see what we would get.

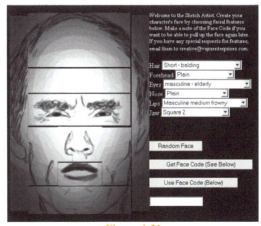

Figure 1.31

Try this out by showing a picture to your students of someone on campus and then have them try and use Sketch Artist to recreate what they saw. You will get some pretty interesting results. Take a look it's really cool!

7. Shape Collage

Have you ever wanted to make a picture collage? Take a look at Shape Collage at **http://www.shapecollage.com/**. It's an automatic photo collage maker. You will need to actually download the software to your machine, but it is well worth it.

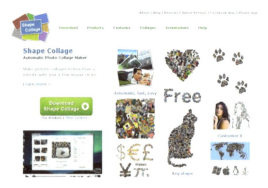

Figure 1.32

As shown in Figure 1.32, just click on the "Download Shape Collage" button and when the dialog box comes up click on "Run". That's all there is to it.

When you open the application it should look like the Figure 1.33.

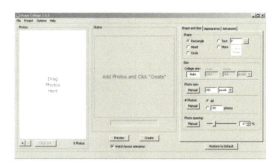

Figure 1.33

It' easy to use; just drag your photos to place them in your collage. The more photos the better. Under the "File" option on the menu you will find that you can add a folder of photos or you can download photos from the Web. I went and got a bunch of them off the web.

On the right side, Figure 1.34, you have some options of how you want your collage to look.

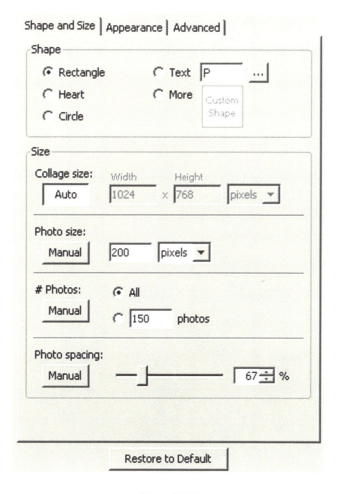

Figure 1.34

We selected the "Heart" and left everything else the same for now. You can see there are a lot of other options to use and experiment with to see how they might affect your collage. We were trying to keep things simple so opted to only change the shape option.

Figure 1.35

The pictures we loaded from shutterstock.com, clicked on create, went through the necessary dialog boxes to save our collage and there is our heart. Here it is saved as a jpeg file.

Figure 1.36

Figure 1.37 shows you can also do a custom shape –

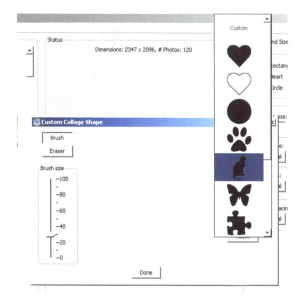

Figure 1.37

When we selected the butterfly – our collage turned out like Figure 1.38.

Figure 1.38

There are a lot of settings you can change to make your collage the way you want it to look. What about a collage of all your students? So this is Wicked Cool!

8. 3DPackage

"3d package is a 3d-box graphic generator. 3d package lets you instantly create 3d-box images online, free! Just upload pictures for cover and sides and then get 3d-box in your favorite image format (JPG, GIF, PNG supported). Post them in your blog or anywhere else."

Figure 1.39

3Dpackage at **http://www.3d-pack.com/** is simple, but neat. It lets you create a three dimensional box. You supply pictures for the sides and it creates a 3-D box graphic image. Figure 1.40 shows our last book.

Figure 1.40

Not only can you do a book, but any of the following.:

Figure 1.41

Once you create your 3-D box image you can save it under the following format.

Figure 1.42

This is Wicked Cool!

9. Picresize

Have you ever wanted to use a photo, but found out it's too large to upload or use? Then you had to find some way to make it smaller or resize it. It just seems that this happens way too often. Picresize at **http://picresize.com** is a good place to solve those problems.

Figure 1.43

All you need do is select the picture you want to resize through the easy to use interface; and then click on the "Continue" button.

This is pretty inclusive as to what it can do. You can crop and rotate your image in step 1. You can resize it in step 2, the deault is 50%, but if you click on the down arrow next to the 50% smaller option you will get several other alternatives. Step 3 will even let you add some special effects.

Figure 1.45

At the bottom of the screen you are presented with options for saving your image. You can select several formats; jpg, gif, png and bmp. When you're ready just click on the "I'm Done, Resize My Picture" button. We just made ours 50% smaller.

Figure 1.46

It will come back and the new size along with several options. We usually select "Save to Disk".

This is an easy to use Wicked Cool tool.

Chapter 2 – Presentations / Slideshows

This category looks at presentation sharing applications and presentation creation applications. Zoho Show, Slide Rocket, Ahead, and Animoto are all presentation sharing and creation tools. Zoho Show and SlideRocket are sort of PowerPoint look alikes, but with some different bells and whistles. Ahead is a whole different way of looking at creating and presenting a presentation. Animoto lets you create a video slideshow using photos, music and video clips.

10. Zoho Show

Have you ever needed to create a presentation? More than likely you have and more than likely you used PowerPoint to create your presentation. Have you wanted to share that presentation with a colleague, but the colleague was located in a different state or country? Wouldn't it be nice if you were able to create a presentation, share that presentation and export that presentation to other presentation management systems and do all this on-line? Now you can. Zoho Show at **http://show.zoho.com** does all of this and more.

Figure 2.1

This is a great tool and easy to use. You will need to sign up, but it is free. You just need to click the new user "Sign Up" option, supply a username and password and you are all set to get started. The "Sign Up" link is on the right side of the screen in the "Sign In" box as can be seen from Figure 2.1. Once you sign up and log in you are presented with an option to create a new presentation or you can import an existing presentation created from another application. If you select the "Create New" option you are presented with the screen shown in Figure 2.2.

Figure 2.2

Here you can give your presentation a name, short description and select a theme. There are a lot of themes to select from so you can easily find one that will suit your needs. We picked "Snowy Stars" under the "Funky" category and filled in the necessary information as can be seen in Figure 2.3. .

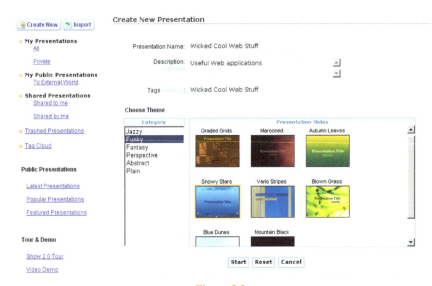

Figure 2.3

Now click on the "Start" button and you are ready to begin. As shown in Figure 2.4 you are now ready to create your first slide, namely your title slide for your presentation.

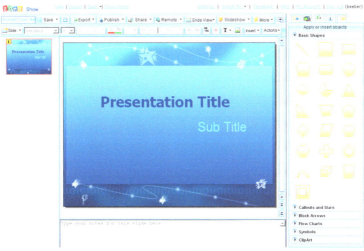

Figure 2.4

You will find that any tool you had available from your previous presentation management system is probably available in Zoho Show. It is missing some bells and whistles, but not many. Yes, it does have slide transitions and animations.

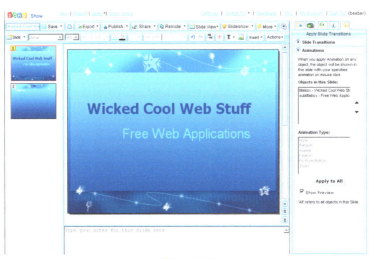

Figure 2.5

When you are done creating your presentation you can export it to a different format or publish it to the web. We have put this right at the top of our list for creating presentations on-line. This is really Wicked Cool!

11. SlideRocket

SlideRocket at **http://www.sliderocket.com** is an on-line presentation management system.

"SlideRocket is a revolutionary new approach to business communications designed from the start to help you make great presentations that engage your audience and deliver tangible results."

Figure 2.6

You will need to sign up; there is both a free version and a pay version. Once you sign up and log in you will be presented with the screen shown in Figure 2.7.

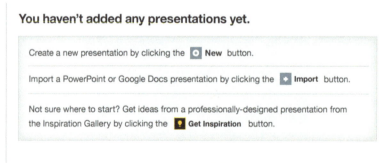

Figure 2.7

You can actually upload an existing presentation and make modifications to it or you can create a presentation from scratch. If you elect to create one from scratch by clicking on the "New" button, you will see the screen shown in Figure 2.8.

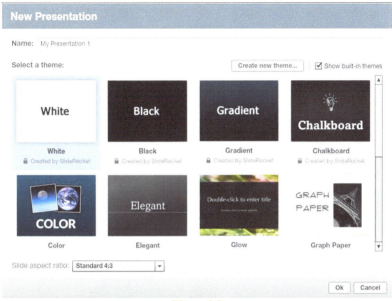

Figure 2.8

You can select an existing theme or create a new one; we selected "Graph Paper". After selecting your theme you are presented with all the necessary tools to create a dynamic presentation.

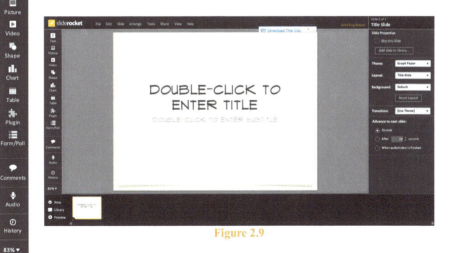

Figure 2.9

Figure 2.10

You will find that the interface is much like that of PowerPoint so it is extremely easy to learn. On the left side you can select from a multitude of items to insert into your slide.

With the free version you won't have access to form/Poll, but everything else should be available. At the top of the screen is a menu with all the usual things you would expect to be in a presentation management system.

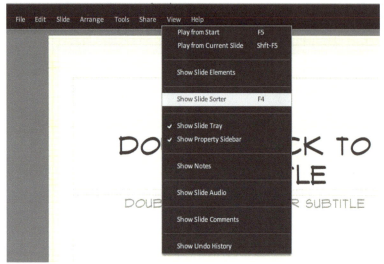

Figure 2.11

This is such a great presentation management system. There are so many things that this offers.
- You can import your presentations.
- You can access your presentation anywhere.
- You can create your presentations on-line.
- You can collaboratively create presentations.
- You can share presentations through several different social media outlets.
- You can create dynamic presentations

What's not to like – this is Wicked Cool!

12. Ahead

Are you tired of those same old PowerPoint presentations? Presentation management is changing. As seen in Figure 2.12, Ahead at **http://ahead.com** is a different way to create and present presentations. "Boost you creativity with Ahead"

Figure 2.12

As stated on their web site "With Ahead you can share and publish content of any kind and any resolution on the web."

You will need to sign up with Ahead, but don't worry it's free and easy to do. Once you are signed up you can log in to begin.

Figure 2.13

Select where you want to go – we selected "Empty Space" and then clicked on "GO".

Figure 2.14

You are now ready to begin creating your presentation. The tools on the left side, Figure 2.15, will let you do most things that you need to do. There are two "add" tools, one will let you upload pictures, media or a document and place it on your workspace. The other will let you insert text on your workspace. After selecting the add media button on the tool bar or the "Media" tab on the menu at the top of the screen, the "My Media" window is displayed. We uploaded a picture by clicking on the "Upload" button and selecting the picture we wanted. Clicking on the "Insert" button placed it on our workspace where we could position and resize it.

Figure 2.15

After you click on the "Insert" button close the "My Media" window so you can see the inserted picture. You can now manipulate the picture.

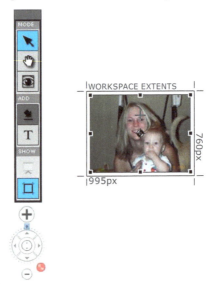

Figure 2.16

As seen in Figure 2.17, you can add text by double clicking anywhere on the workspace.

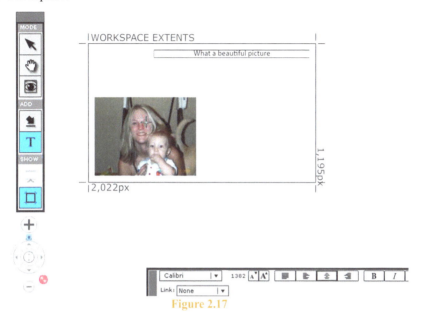

Figure 2.17

You can easily change the text by using the text tool bar which appears when the text is selected.

Now that we know how to insert media and text in our workspace, let's see if we can get a handle on how things work. The workspace is divided into three layers; front, zoom and back. The front layer contains stationary items that you want to appear on top of your presentation. The back layer also contains stationary media and text, but it's in the background of your workspace. The zoom layer or main layer contains media and text that can be zoomed to during your presentation. To select between the layers and in turn place media and text on the different layers click on the "Tools" icon in the upper right of the screen; this will open the advanced menu. The tabs on the right in Figure 2.18 are for switching between the three layers. When you have selected a layer you can place media and text on it by using the add tools for inserting media and text. Remember front and back are stationary and the zoom layer you can pan and zoom. The layering idea takes a little time to figure out, but we think it really has some potential when it comes to creating some really dynamic presentations. It's a little like layering in Photoshop. So let's put something on each of the three layers.

Figure 2.18

We put text on the front and back layers and three pictures, all the same, on the zoom layer. See Figure 2.19.

Figure 2.19

Figure 2.19 shows what is on the front layer. If we click on the back layer tab it would show the text "This is the back layer" and if we click on the zoom tab it would show the three pictures. So basically you can put anything you want on any layer. Remember the only layer that you can zoom or pan is the zoom layer.

Next we break our workspace, zoom layer, into scenes. You will find the scene tool on the toolbar on the left. Once selected, you can place a rectangle around that part of the zoom layer that you want to be considered a scene, think of it as a slide in a presentation. See Figure 2.20.

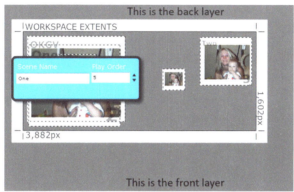

Figure 2.20

We placed a scene around each of our pictures naming them one, two and three. The play order is the order the scenes will be seen. Anything you can place a rectangle around can be a scene. So we added one more scene by placing a rectangle around just the face in the large picture.

Figure 2.21

In Figure 2.21 you can see from the dotted lines where the scenes are.

You're now ready to play your presentation. Select the view button at the top of the screen. Figure 2.22 shows the view button.

Figure 2.22

It's the button next to the tools button. You are now ready to start presenting.

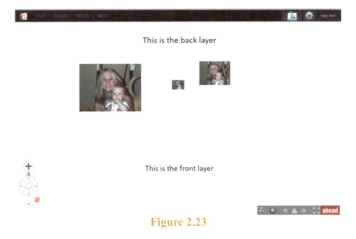

Figure 2.23

At the bottom, Figure 2.23, you can click on the left and right arrows to zoom to a different scene. Start by clicking on home to get to your beginning scene. The four slides from our presentation follow in figures 2.24, 2.25,2.26 and 2.27.

Figure 2.24

Figure 2.25

Figure 2.26

Figure 2.27

We probably should have used a different picture each time, but hopefully you get the idea. The media on the front and back layer always remain in the same place. The zoom layer zooms in the scenes we created. There is a lot you can do with this presentation management system. It does take a little time to get used to it, but it is well worth it. There is no option to save your presentation locally, but you can save it to the Ahead web site and have access to it via internet at all times. This is Wicked Cool!

13. Animoto

Animoto at **http://animoto.com** uses photos, video and music to let you make a super cool slideshow presentation.

Figure 2.28

You will need to sign up to use Animoto, but it is well worth it, and it's free. Animoto is a presentation generator whose focus is on using images to create your presentation. Once you have signed up with Animoto and logged in click on the "Create Video" button in the upper right of the screen to get started.

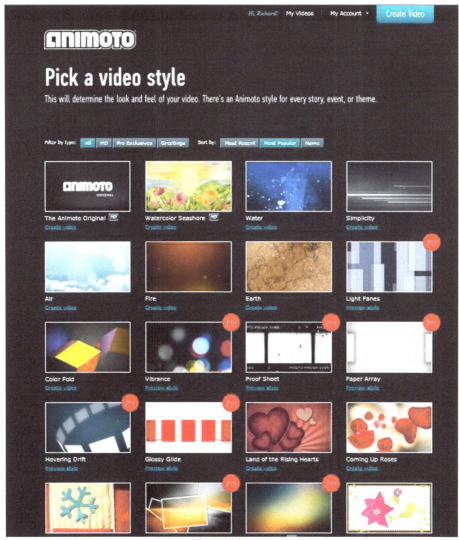

Figure 2.29

As shown in Figure 2.29 you will be presented with several video styles to choice from. You can only choice those that do not have the word "Pro" by them. Several versions of Animoto are available; paid versions and a free version. The free version is limited to a thirty second presentation and certain video styles. We selected the Animoto original by clicking on the "Create video" link under our selection.

Figure 2.30

After the window in Figure 2.30 comes up, click on the "make a 30 second video for free" link on the lower right hand side.

Figure 2.31

As shown in Figure 2.31, this is really super easy; start by selecting the images or short video clips that you want to include in your presentation. You have several options of where to retrieve the images and videos from; your computer, facebook, a website, or you can used those from Animoto. We clicked on the "Upload" option and selected some photos of our own. You can select multiple photos by using the ctrl and shift key as you are selecting them.

Figure 2.32

Remember you are limited to a thirty second video so don't get carried away with the number of photos. We didn't add any, but you can also upload small five second videos to include in your presentation. By selecting the tools at the bottom you can add text, rotate, spotlight, delete, shuffle, and if needed add more photos. See Figure 2.32.
Next click the music tab to add your music to your video.

Figure 2.33

We selected some music provided by Animoto. Last click on the "Finalize" tab or the "Continue" button.

Figure 2.34

If you are happy with what you have click on "Continue".

Figure 2.35

Figure 2.35 shows the screen where you can supply a name, description and author for your video presentation; when you're done click the "Create Video" button". Animoto will present you with the screen in Figure 2.36.

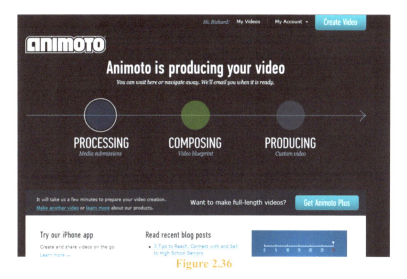

Figure 2.36

After a short period of time your video will be processed and you will be presented with the screen in Figure 2.37.

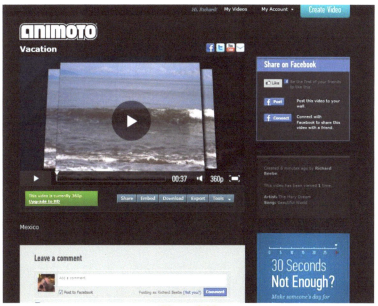

Figure 2.37

Here you have options to download or share your video. To play your video just click on the "Play button.

Figure 2.38

Figure 2.38 shows a capture of the video playing. If you click on the "My Videos" at the top you will see all your videos that have been created.

Figure 2.39

This tool would be great for class collaboration. We think this is the Wickedest!

Chapter 3 – Shared Document Creation

There are those times when you want to create a document collaboratively. Maybe it's a project for school or work or maybe it's a situation where everyone working on the document cannot be in the same place. Either way here are some applications that fit into this category.

- TypeWithMe will let multiple people type and create a document at the same time.

- CoSketch is an online whiteboard where multiple users can place images and text – great place to share ideas.

- TinyChat is an online chat application that is very easy to use.

There are so many times when we need to share things. What could be easier than using these applications? Besides they are free to use. So cool.

14. Typewith.me

Typewith.me at **http://www.typewith.me** is a really interesting idea –

Figure 3.1

When you select "Click to Create a New Document" you will get a document which will allow you to interact with other users. See Figure 3.2.

Figure 3.2

All you need to do is send the link (url) to whoever you want to be able to type with you. You can invite others simply by copying the link (url) and sending via your email or you can click on the "Invite" option or "Share this" button and email it that way – it's really easy to do.

When you start typing, each author's text is color coded so you can tell who's adding what. You can select your color by clicking on the color icon next to "<enter your name>". Text is somewhat limited as to what you can do with it; basically you can bold, italicize, underline and strikethrough.

Figure 3.3

Not only can you be sharing in the writing of your document, but you can also be using a chat room to aid in the collaboration of the document. When you're done you can remove the author colors through the "option" menu and then save your document under several different formats using the "Import/export" menu.

To save time you can also import from several different formats, like Word, HTML or a TXT file.

This is a fantastic web site – easy to use with a lot of potential for collaborative creation of documents. It's definitely Wicked Cool.

15. CoSketch

CoSketch is a multi-user online whiteboard designed to give you the ability to quickly visualize and share your ideas as images. Take a look at **http://cosketch.com**.

Figure 3.4

Click on the "create a sketch" link. You should see the screen in Figure 3.5.

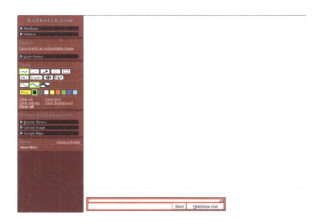

Figure 3.5

What you have is a multiuser sketch pad. Just send the url to anyone that you want to use it with you. As seen in Figure 3.6 there are some pretty interesting tools that you can use.

Figure 3.6

You have line, arrow, circle and rectangle tools along with text and being able to move and rotate. You can also change color. One of the neater things is the Library, Figure 3.7.

Figure 3.7

Here you can find some interesting "stamps" to use, Figure 3.8.

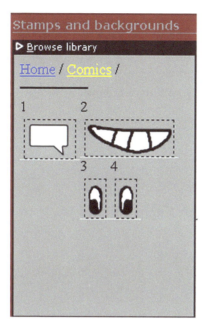

Figure 3.8

You can also upload your own image or use Google maps; all of this in a multiuser environment. You can also chat with the users working on the sketch. When you are done you can save your image via an embedded link or download it as an image.

Figure 3.9

This is a wicked cool multiuser whiteboard.

16. TinyChat

You will love this, a free video chat room. Create a chat-room on-the-fly and share the URL with others (no email address needed). Then when you're done, download the completed chat as an RTF file. Take a look at TinyChat at **http://www.Tinychat.com**.

Figure 3.10

To use this is really easy – simply click on the "Create a Room" button. You will need an account, but it is free.

"Tinychat provides dead simple, free to use, video chat rooms that just work! Enjoy chatting with your friends or making new ones, just create a chat room or join one."

What is Tinychat?

Tinychat provides dead simple, free to use, video chat rooms that just work! Enjoy chatting with your friends or making new ones, just create a chat room or join one

Figure 3.11

Once you have an account click on the "create a chat room" at the bottom of the screen.

Figure 3.12

As seen in Figure 3.12, you can sign in to your Facebook or Twitter accounts, or just click on Go to use your Tinychat account.

Figure 3.13

You will be prompted for a room topic and some information about who can use the room, Figure 3.13.

Figure 3.24

When you click on OK, you are ready to begin. Just click on the "Start Broadcasting" button, Figure 3.24. You will be given some options about what you want to use to broadcast such as a microphone or a video camera.

Figure 3.25

Once setup you are all set to go. Just send the url to those who you want to be included in your Tinychat room.

Really Wicked Cool!

Chapter 4 – Text Creations

This category deals with taking words or characters and creating different shapes from them. There are some really interesting results that can be obtained. In some cases, such as Wordle, we can determine most and least used words. Wordsift tries to visualize text, which is a fantastic concept. Tagxedo creates what are called word clouds. In this category we have also included Typemirror, which is a text manipulation application. PhoneSpell creates words from phone numbers and Text-Image creates a text or ascii representation of a picture. We could have also included Text-Image in Chapter 1 on Photo and Paint.

These are applications that can be used in some interesting ways. Let your imagination and creativity lead the way.

17. Wordle

There are some really interesting things that people think up. Wordle at **http://www.wordle.net**, falls into one of those interesting things categories. When we first came across this web site, we thought it was really cool, but couldn't put a handle on using it. We were so mistaken. The Wordle website describes wordle as follows:

"Wordle is a toy for generating "word clouds" from text that you provide. The clouds give greater prominence to words that appear more frequently in the source text. You can tweak your clouds with different fonts, layouts, and color schemes. The images you create with Wordle are yours to use however you like. You can print them out, or save them to the Wordle gallery to share with your friends."

Word clouds are exactly what you might think; creating clouds from text that you provide.

Figure 4.1

The clouds give greater prominence to words that appear more frequently in the source text. So by selecting text over the same topics you can make some interesting designs. What's more it's a great way to make a point or display a list of topics that might be on an upcoming exam, if you're a teacher.

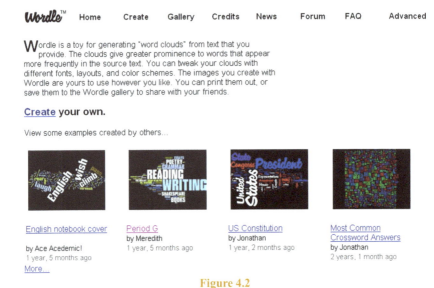

Figure 4.2

To create a wordle is super easy. Click on "Create" to begin

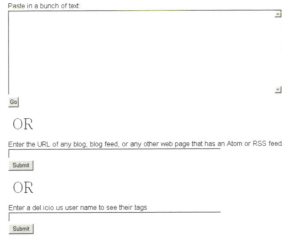

Figure 4.3

As seen in Figure 4.3 you have several options for supplying the text. You can type it in, copy and paste, enter a URL to a blog or grab back the tags by entering a del.icio.us name. It's really simple to use. We selected some text from the wordle web site. When you're done click on the "Go" or "Submit" button to create your wordle.

Figure 4.4

You can see it created a pretty interesting wordle, Figure 4.4. You not only can remove certain types of words, but by selecting "Font" from the menu; you can change the layout of the text, making the words more rounded or mostly horizontal and you can also change the color scheme being used to display the text. There are a lot of combinations to try. When you're done you can print your wordle to a printer or use a screen capture utility to capture.

With a little thought and imagination we think you will find wordle to be a really Wicked Cool web site.

18. Wordsift

Have you ever wanted to visualize text? WordSift at **http://www.wordsift.com** will let you do just that.

Figure 4.5

There is no login or sign up necessary to use Wordsift. Wordsift is best described by the web site itself.

"WordSift was created to help teachers manage the demands of vocabulary and academic language in their text materials. We especially hope that this tool is helpful in supporting English Language Learners. We want WordSift to be a useful tool, but we also want it to be fun and visually pleasing. We would be happy if you think of it playfully - as a toy in a linguistic playground that is available to instantly capture and display the vocabulary structure of texts, and to help create an opportunity to talk and explore the richness and wonders of language!

WordSift helps anyone easily sift through texts -- just cut and paste any text into WordSift and you can engage in a verbal quick-capture! The program helps to quickly identify important words that appear in the text. This function is widely available in various Tag Cloud programs on the web, but we have added the ability to mark and sort different lists of words important to educators. We have also integrated it with a few other functions, such as visualization of word thesaurus relationships (incorporating the amazing Visual Thesaurus® that we highly recommend in its own right) and Google® searches of images and videos. With just a click on any word in the Tag Cloud, the program displays instances of sentences in which that word is used in the text."

All you need do is copy some text into Wordsift and click on the "sift" button. We copied the above text into Wordsift pressed the "sift" button and got some cool results, Figure 4.6.

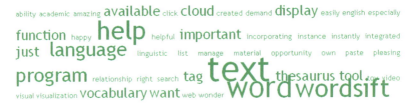

At the top of the screen you will get a word cloud, with the more common text emphasized. You can change the order of text by selecting one of the options "Common to Rare", "Rare to Common", "A to Z" or "Z to A". You can also have particular categories of words marked by selecting Math or Science or one of the other options. So basically the top part of the screen gives you a word cloud that you can reorder and mark text. That's pretty cool, but there is so much more.

If you click on any word in the word cloud, a Goggle search will be done for videos and web sites that might pertain to that word. See Figure 4.7 to see what we got when we selected "Word" in the word cloud.

Figure 4.7

The other neat thing here is you also get a visual thesaurus of the word. See Figure 4.8.

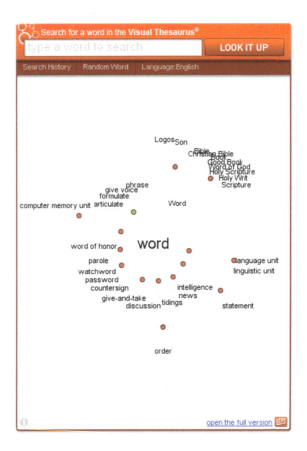

Figure 4.8

The use of this is limited only by your imagination. We think you will find lots of uses for this application. We have used it several times to get a visual look at a word. This is a Wicked Cool tool.

19. Tagxedo

What a simple idea, Tagxedo at **http://www.tagxedo.com/** calls it "tag cloud with styles". It is really a great idea, take a word cloud and create it within a shape.

"turn words -- famous speeches, news articles, slogans and themes, even your love letters -- into a visually stunning tag cloud, words individually sized appropriately to highlight the frequencies of occurrence within the body of text."

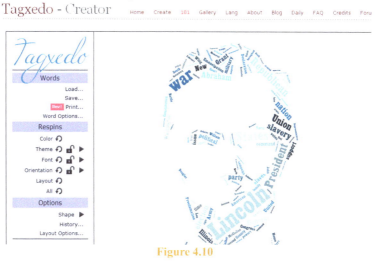

Figure 4.9

There are a lot of options to put text into Tagxedo to create your word cloud shape. You can actually make a word cloud shape from your blog or any tweets, but let's click on the "StartNow" button or the "create" tab to get to a place where we can paste some text into our word cloud.

Figure 4.10

To load in your own text, click on the "Load" option, Figure 4.10. You will get the load menu, Figure 4.11.

Load Menu   X

File: Browse...

Webpage: [   ]   Submit

Enter Text: [   ]   Submit

             Hint: Ctrl-A to select all, Ctrl-C to copy, Ctrl-V to paste

Player (XAP): Browse...

Figure 4.11

You can paste text or type it in, it's your choice. We copied some text and pasted it into the load menu. It seemed to be the fastest way. After you paste in your text select "Submit" to create your word cloud, Figure 4.12.

Figure 4.12

You can use the options on the left side of the screen to change the color, theme, font, orientation and layout of the text, Figure 4.13.

Figure 4.13

To place your text in a shape, select the arrow to the right of the "Shape" option.

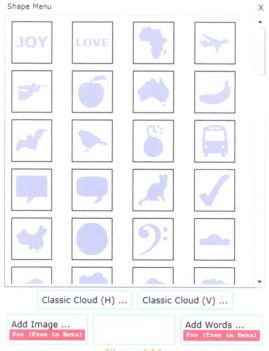

Figure 4.14

You can now select a shape for your newly created word cloud, Figure 4.14. We scrolled down and selected the heart.

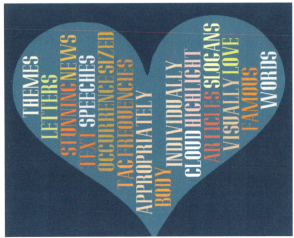

Figure 4.15

You can also alter the layout options by selecting "Layout options", Figure 4.16.

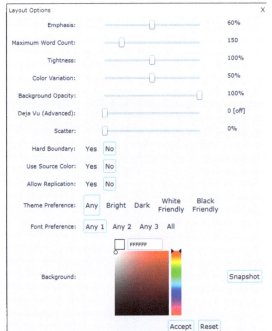

Figure 4.16

Once you are done creating your master piece take a look at the "save" option. You can save your Tagxedo in just about any format, Figure 4.17.

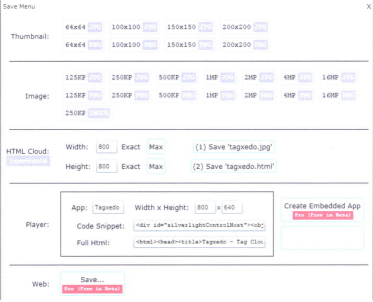

Figure 4.17

You can also print your tagxedo. Tagxedo is a really great idea with a lot of possibilities. On their web site they have 101 ways to use Tagxedo. This is really a Wicked Cool tool.

20. Typemirror

There are a few web sites that do some of the same things as **http://typemirror.com/**, but what makes Typemirror stand out is that it does more than just one text manipulation. With Typemirror you can actually do three different things. Reverse text does exactly that, type in your text and it will let you copy the text in reverse. Brokencaps will give you a random upper and lower case text back and Rainbow text will change each letter to a different color. Both reverse text and Brokencaps text can be copied and pasted, Rainbow text can be placed in a web page by copying the code provided. Figure 4.18 shows their beginning page.

Figure 4.18

How it works is pretty easy – select the option you want to use. We selected "Reversed Text", Figure 4.19.

Figure 4.19

Type the text you want reversed and click on the "Submit" button, Figure 4.20.

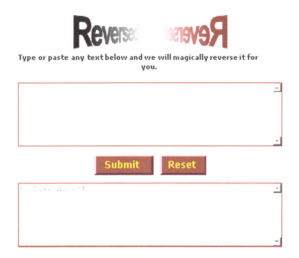

Figure 4.20

Now that it's reversed you can copy and paste it anywhere. The Broken Caps option works the same way. If you want something with a little more bells and whistles then look at something like Rainbow Text, Figure 4.21.

Figure 4.21

Figure 4.22 shows what you get when you press the "Submit" button.

Figure 4.22

To place this in a document you will need to copy the code. This works for anyplace that will let you place HTML. We have used this several times. It's Wicked Cool.

21. Words from telephone numbers

Have you ever wondered what your telephone number spells? Have you ever wanted to pick a new telephone number, but wanted to pick one that spells something? Phonespell at **http://www.phonespell.org** will tell you what your phone number spells.

Figure 4.23

Just type in your phone number and Phonespell will give you all the things it spells. We typed in 4739, Figure 4.24.

Figure 4.24

We also typed in 732, Figure 4.25

Words starting with telephone number prefix 732

We found these 7-letter words:

```
peaches (732-2437)    peacock (732-2625)    peafowl (732-3695)
peaking (732-5464)    pealing (732-5464)    peanuts (732-6887)
pearler (732-7537)    peasant (732-7268)    pebbled (732-2533)
pebbles (732-2537)    peccary (732-2279)    pecking (732-5464)
reached (732-2433)    reacher (732-2437)    reaches (732-2437)
reacted (732-2833)    reactor (732-2867)    readers (732-3377)
readied (732-3433)    readier (732-3437)    readies (732-3437)
readily (732-3459)    reading (732-3464)    readout (732-3688)
reagent (732-4368)    realest (732-5378)    realign (732-5446)
realism (732-5476)    realist (732-5478)    reality (732-5489)
realize (732-5493)    realtor (732-5867)    reaming (732-6464)
reaping (732-7464)    rearing (732-7464)    rearmed (732-7633)
reasons (732-7667)    rebated (732-2833)    rebater (732-2837)
rebates (732-2837)    Rebecca (732-3222)    Rebekah (732-3524)
rebells (732-3557)    rebirth (732-4784)    rebonds (732-6637)
reboots (732-6687)    rebound (732-6863)    rebuffs (732-8337)
rebuild (732-8453)    rebuilt (732-8458)    rebuked (732-8533)
rebuker (732-8537)    rebukes (732-8537)    recalls (732-2557)
recasts (732-2787)    receded (732-3333)    recedes (732-3337)
receipt (732-3478)    receive (732-3483)    recency (732-3629)
recheck (732-4325)    recipes (732-4737)    recital (732-4825)
recited (732-4833)    reciter (732-4837)    recites (732-4837)
reckons (732-5667)    reclaim (732-5246)    recline (732-5463)
recluse (732-5873)    recoded (732-6333)    recodes (732-6337)
```

Figure 4.25 1

Which gave us a lot of different combinations.

"Use this search to help you select a new telephone number with a memorable mnemonic. Ask your local telephone company or mobile phone service provider if they can get this number for you in your area code. If you have a business, ask your long distance provider if they can get this phone number for you as toll free number so your customers can easily remember how to reach you." This is Wicked Cool!

22. www.text-image.com

Have you ever wanted to create a text image from a picture? Well I didn't either. That is until I found Text-Image at **http://www.text-image.com**. As stated on their web site "Here you can easily generate cool text-images from almost any picture you have on your computer".

Figure 4.26

Click on the "Convert" tab to begin, Figure 4.27.

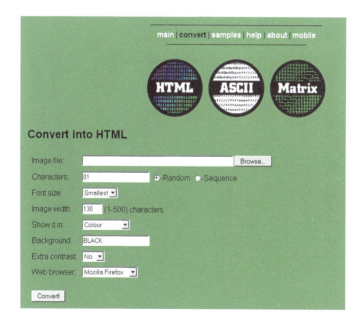

Figure 4.27

Find a picture to use and click on the "Convert" button at the bottom of the screen. Here's the original picture, Figure 4.28.

Figure 4.28

Here it is as a Matrix rendering, Figure 4.29.

Figure 4.29

Here it is as an HTML rendering, Figure 4.30.

Figure 4.30

And finally as a ASCII rendering, Figure 4.31.

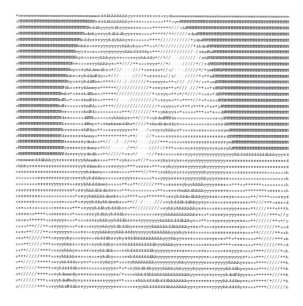

Figure 4.31

Each of these has options that you can change to get different looks –
personally we like the ASCII rendering the best. This is Wicked Cool!

Chapter 5 – Fun Stuff

Sometimes we just like to show our students some web stuff that's not necessarily all that useful, instead it's just fun to think about what you might use them for. There are a lot of possibilities, but generally it's just fun to get that wow factor.

- Some things are just meant to be different. Star Wars is an example of text animation. It's an example of creating a full length movie using ascii characters. It's one of those things you need to see to fully appreciate it.
- Alice is a chat bot. We have shown this several times, and it always seems to achieve that wow factor. The web is so great.
- Warning Sign Generator is exactly what the name implies. It will let you create any type of warning sign. We placed it here in the fun category because when we show it to our classes they generally use it to create really bazaar warning signs.
- Prison Name Generator sort of says it all. Have you ever wondered what your nickname would be if you ended up in prison? We actually didn't wonder either, on the other hand Prison Name Generator will definitely make you laugh. We do want to state a warning about this application in that the nick names it generates are sometimes a little in the R to X rated arena.

23. Star Wars

Ok, so sometimes we just want to see something that is just plain out and out Wicked Cool. So here it is, start by doing the following –

- Click on the start button – in the search box type telnet.
- At the telnet prompt type
- Open towel.blinkenlights.nl
- Enjoy the movie

Yup a movie. This is a Star Wars movie completely done in Ascii. This is a must see, Figure 5.1.

The author of this ascii animation has also created a web site at **http://asciimation.co.nz/** which has a few updates to the original. So if you have the time, watch an ascii animation star wars movie. Wicked Cool!!

Figure 5.1

24. Alice

Figure 5.2

Have you ever wanted to talk to a chat Bot? What's a chat bot? A robot designed to talk to humans about various subjects. Take a look at ALICE, ask her questions, carry on a conversation with her, you can even get personal with her. This is one of the many off-shoots of artificial intelligence. Alice at **http://www.pandorabots.com/pandora/talk?botid=f5d922d97e345aa1** is Wicked Cool.

25. Warning sign generator

Have you ever had a time when you wanted to create a warning sign? Well here's a tool which will let you do exactly that. Warning sign generator at

http://www.warningsigngenerator.com/ is easy to use and lets you create about any warning sign you can imagine, Figure 5.3.

Figure 5.3

Start by selecting your warning sign – we selected the third one in the first row.

Figure 5.4

Next select a warning symbol – we selected wheel chair, Figure 5.5.

Figure 5.5

Finally type in your warning message.

Figure 5.6

Click on generate your warning message, Figure 5.6.

Figure 5.7

All done, just right click on the image and click on "save picture as". This is Wicked Cool.

26. Prison Name Generator

This is just interesting and fun, so we thought it would certainly fit in this category. Prison Name Generator at **http://www.prisonbitchname.com/** is simple, but neat. Again, we want to warn you that some of the names it generates are not appropriate for all ages.

Figure 5.8

It's easy enough to use, simply type in your first and last name and click on the "Submit Button", your prison name will be generated. Wicked Cool!

Chapter 6 – Discussions

These are great tools; they let you share your ideas by placing them on the web and promoting collaboration with others. Voxopop is an online message board that lets you place the messages as audio messages in your own voice. Glogster, what a need word, is a blog, but with a twist, you can mix graphics, photos, videos, music and text. Wallwisher is really cool. Wallwisher is an on line notice board maker - a really neat idea.

27. Voxopop

Have you ever used an online message board or been part of an online discussion board? Well Voxopop at **http://www.voxopop.com/** takes the concept a step further. Instead of typing your message or adding to the discussion by typing your response, Voxopop lets you say what you want in your own voice. As Voxopop's web site says "Used by educators all over the world, Voxopop talkgroups are a fun, engaging and easy-to-use way to help students develop their speaking skills. They're a bit like message boards, but use voice rather than text and have a specialized user interface. No longer confined to a physical classroom, teachers and students of oral skills can interact from home, or even from opposite sides of the planet!
Anywhere. Anytime.".

Figure 6.1

You will need to create an account to be able to add to a group discussion or create your own group, but again remember it's free. You can get a pretty good idea of what Voxopop is like by clicking on the Explore Talk Groups and Discussions tab.

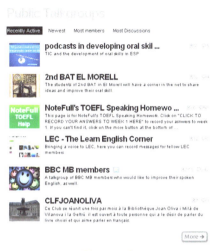

Figure 6.2

Click on any of the public talkgroups to see what it's like. We clicked on "podcasts in developing oral skills", Figure 6.3.

Figure 6.3

After clicking on one of the general discussion options, we selected "How can podcasts help in the development or oral skills?"; you will be able to listen to the discussions, Figure 6.4.

Figure 6.4

Simply click on any discussion message to listen or select the "Play All" tab to listen to everything. You can also add your own two cents by selecting the "Record a Message" button. It's really pretty interesting to actually listen to someone rather than reading the response. If you want to create your own discussion group, select the "Start a Talk Group" tab at the top of the page. You will be prompted to fill out the necessary information for the creation of your group.

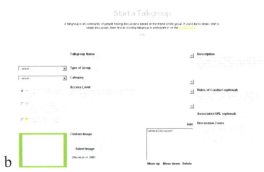

Figure 6.5

When you are done filling everything in select the "Create my Talkgroup" tab at the bottom of the page this will create your talk group and allow others to use it, Figure 6.6.

Figure 6.6

You are the admin for the group, so you probably want to create an introductory message telling what the group is about. You can also invite others to join your discussion. If this was a class you could invite your students to join the discussion. That's all there is to it. This adds a whole new dimension to the idea of discussion groups and message boards. Message boards with real voices; you can create a public or a private talkgroup and you can be notified when others contribute to your talkgroup (keep a watchlist). This is definitely a Wicked Cool web site.

28. Glogster

Everyone seems to know what a blog is, but do you know what a glog is? It's a blog, but with a twist; you can mix graphics, photos, videos, music and text. Hence, this is where the name glog comes from. Take a look at Glogster at **http://www.glogster.com**.

Figure 6.7

On the Globster web site they have several reasons for using a glob:

Figure 6.8

To create a glob click on the "Try To Create Yours" button.

Figure 6.9

You are now ready to add different media to create your glog. You can click on any of the items on the magnet tool to have access to a variety of different media that you can add to your glog, Figure 6.10.

Figure 6.10

Even after the item is place on your wall you can edit it my clicking on it and selecting what you want to do with it, Figure 6.11.

Figure 6.11

Once you are done you can publish your glob for everyone to see. So next time you think about creating a blog, you might consider a glob instead, kind of an enhanced blog. This is another Wicked Cool web site.

29. Wallwisher

Have you ever wanted someplace to post notices about events or just a place to post stuff for your class to read or lookup? Will that's exactly what Wallwisher at **http://www.wallwisher.com** is for. The folks at Wallwisher claim it is a "new way to communicate". So basically Wallwisher is an online "notice board" maker.

Figure 6.12

If you take a look at the demo wall you can a quick feel for what Wallwisher is all about, Figure 6.13.

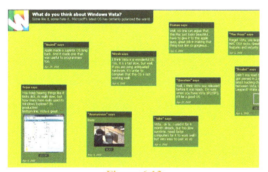

Figure 6.13

Notes can be posted on the wall and can contain not only text but also pictures and videos. To create your own Wallwisher wall is pretty painless. Just click on "Build a wall" at the top of the screen, Figure 6.14.

Figure 6.14

You simply add a title, subtitle and maybe a picture to give an idea of what your wall is all about. Choose the URL and designate who can view and post to your wall. You can even approve posting by others before they appear on your wall. Pick a Theme for the background and color scheme for your wall. Last, type in your email and name. Click on the Done button in the lower right corner and your wall is created. They will email you instructions on how to edit and manage your wall. Here's the email. We did remove our username and password, Figure 6.15.

Figure 6.15

After you log in with the password they send you, you will be at your wall. To add a note just double click anywhere on the screen, Figure 6.16.

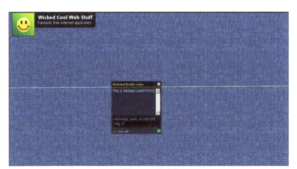

Figure 6.16

You can add text, images, audio or video. Anyone you send the link to can post to your wall. This is really cool. This is Wicked Cool!

Chapter 7 – Tools

There are a lot of tools available to use on the web. By tools we mean those applications which just make things easier to do or maybe something that will help you in doing something else. In this category we have included some really simple applications that have helped to make things easier.

- Bibme, what a great tool. Bibme creates a bibliography for you and you can select the format you want need. We wish we had this tool years ago.
- Howjsay will pronounce a word or phrase for you. There have been a lot of times when we were not sure how to pronounce something. Now we can use Howjsay to find out.
- ZimZar lets you change a file to a different format. We can only begin to remember how many times we have had to do this. What a life saver.
- Downforeveryoneorjustme is a tool to determine if the web site you are trying to get to is really down. When you are not sure if it's on your end or it's the web site itself.

30. Bibme

How many times have you had to make a bibliography? I can remember the pains- taking process of gathering up all the information and then trying to put it in the necessary format. We always had to look up the different formats for APA and MLA. Even with a MLA or APA reference manual in hand, most of the time we formatted it wrong. Then there was always the problem of finding the book we were referencing, because we took it back to the library. Well those problems have been eliminated with bibme at **http://bibme.org**.

Figure 7.1

All you need is the ISBN number and Bibme will create your reference for you in the format you want. This has got to be one of the best things since sliced bread. Just type in the ISBN number; click on the "Find Book" button and your good to go, Figure 7.2.

Figure 7.2

Click on the green select check mark to see all the book info, Figure 7.3.

Figure 7.3

You can make changes if necessary. Then when you are ready, click on the "Add to My Bibliography" button at the bottom of the page. On the right side of the screen you will see your newly created bibliography, as in Figure 7.4.

Figure 7.4

It's easy enough to change to a different format, just use the pull down menu next to format. To download your newly created bibliography you will need an account, but it is free so all is good.

One of the great things about this web site is that it's not just limited to books; you can also create bibliographies for magazines, newspapers, and just about everything. Just click on the tab for what you want to create a bibliography for.

Figure 7.5

We have used this web site many times, and each time it has been a life saver. It is a Wicked Cool web site. Bibme says it all "The fully automatic bibliography maker that auto-fills. It's the easiest way to build a works cited page. **And it's free.**"

31. HowJSay

Have you ever had a word you were not sure how to pronounce? If only someone could help you out. Well here's a great web site which will pronounce more than 100,000 different words. Take a look a Howjsay at **http://howjsay.com/**.

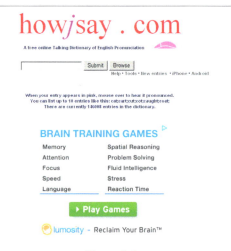

Figure 7.6

It's easy to use, just type in the word you want it to pronounce, Figure 7.7.

Figure 7.7

You can even translate a word to different languages. It won't actually say it in a different language it just translates it, Figure 7.8.

It's so simple and easy to use; what a Böse Cool tool.

32. Zamzar

Have you ever wanted to convert files to a different format without the need to download software? Take a look at Zamzar at **http://www.zamzar.com/**.

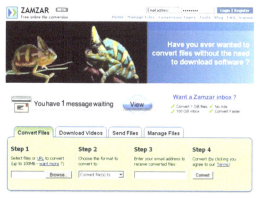

Figure 7.9

This is very easy to use. Just select the file you want to convert. Select what you want to convert it to, supply your e-mail address and click on convert. The file will be converted to the format you select and emailed to the email address you have supplied. The only drawback is that it is limited to 100MB files unless you upgrade to a paid service. On the plus side you will find that your choices of what you can convert to are pretty extensive. Wicked Cool!

33. Downforeveryoneorjustme

Have you ever gone to a web site and it doesn't come up or you get and error stating that the web site you are trying to go to is unavailable? We are sure this has happened to most of us, we know it has happened to us many times. Our first thought is always – why are they down when we want to go there? Then we wonder if they are really down or is it just our connection. Here's a neat web application which is simple and to the point. It just tells you if it's you or if the web site really is down. Take a look at downforeveryoneorjustme at
http://www.downforeveryoneorjustme.com/

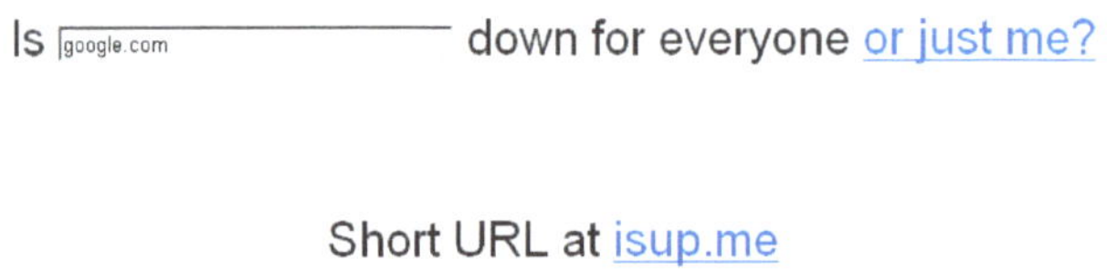

Is ⎸google.com⎹ down for everyone or just me?

Short URL at isup.me

Figure 7.10

Type in the URL and click on "or just me?", Figure 7.11 tells us the web site is up.

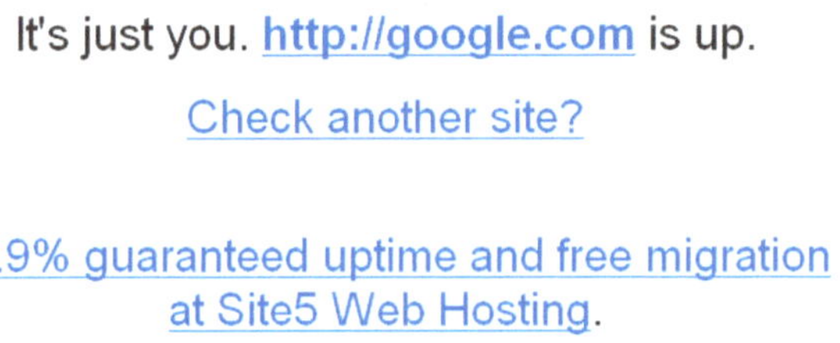

It's just you. http://google.com is up.

Check another site?

99.9% guaranteed uptime and free migration at Site5 Web Hosting.

Figure 7.11

We have our answer. It's simple and to the point, and it is Wicked Cool.

Chapter 8 – Reminders

In this category we have placed those applications which remind us to do something, or possibly remind others to do what we have asked.Wakerupper and Monkeyonyourback are two such tools. Wakerupper is a reminder tool that calls us on the phone and reminds us of some event. Actually you can have it call your own phone or someone else's at a specified time. Now that could be interesting.

Monkeyonyourback uses any valid email as its vehicle mechanism to remind you or someone else of an event. We have also included FreePhoneTracer in this category; it's not really a reminder application, but it will let you find the location of a phone number, so if you need to find out where a phone call originated from you could use FreePhoneTracer and then send them a reminder using Wakerupper.

34. Wakerupper

Have you ever been somewhere and needed someone to call you on your phone as a reminder, or maybe a wakeup call. "Wakerupper is the web's easiest telephone reminder tool. Schedule reminder calls on the web."

Take a look at Wakerupper at **http://wakerupper.com/**.

Figure 8.1

It's easy to use; just give a time when you want a call, a phone number to call, and a short message of what you want the call to say.

Featured Press

Wakerupper was chosen by TIME.com editors as one of the 50 Best Websites of 2010.

"Wakerupper is a simple site with a profound service."
-Time.com

Figure 8.2 1

Wicked Cool!

35. Monkey on Your Back

Need to remind someone to do something for you? Wouldn't it be nice if you could send them a reminder? Take a look at Monkey on Your Back at **http://monkeyon.com**.

Figure 8.3

You will need to sign up to use it, but no worries it's free. Once you sign up you are ready to begin.

Figure 8.4

You can send a monkey as a reminder to any valid e-mail address. It also keeps track of sent reminders and reminders that others have sent you.

So this is definitely a tool I could use for my students. This is Wicked Cool.

36. Freephonetracer

Have you ever gotten that missed phone call and wanted to find out who it was? Freephonetracer at **http://www.freephonetracer.com/** will do a free trace on any valid phone number.

Figure 8.5

When you type in a phone number you will get the information as seen in Figure 8.6.

Figure 8.6

It even located us via our cell phone number. If you want to find out more there is a cost, butf or a simple locator it works great, and it's free. It's Wicked Cool.

Chapter 9 – Cartoons and Comics

Cartoons and comic strips are such a fun way to communicate. They have been around forever. As we stated in our first book "Wicked Cool Web Stuff", "What better way to get your point across and be entertaining at the same time." Here we have expanded this category to include all applications dealing with creating static and animated cartoon characters to creating static and animated comic strips.

- Caricaturesoft will let you upload a photo and very quickly convert it to a cartoon-looking character.
- Comeeko lets you create a comic strip using your own photos. Think of all the possibilities.
- Myths and Legends is really cool; you can tell a story using comic strips. All the tools and images you use are available as part of the Myths and Legends application.
- Blabberize animates a picture and lets you add your voice, so it looks like the picture is talking.
- Fluxtime also lets you create an animated comic. What a great way to tell a story.
- Scratch is an easy-to-use programming language that you can use to create animated comics. Totally fun to do.
- Fuzzwich is by far one of the easier to use Web based animated cartoon creators.
- Voki lets you create your very own talking avatar. This is truly a fun application that we have used on many occasions.

We think you will really enjoy these. You will think of so many different ways to use them; remember you're only limited by your imagination.

37. Caricaturesoft

This is a simple to use application that converts photos to cartoons. You can download the software, or you can use an online version. The downloaded version gives you a few more features that the online version doesn't have, but the downloaded version is limited to ten conversions. After that you need to purchase the software if you want to continue using it. When you visit Caracaturesoft at **http://www.caricaturesoft.com/** you will see the screen shown in Figure 9.1. The menu at the top will let you select the "Download" option where you can download the software and use it, or you can click on the "Online Tools" option and use the online version.

Figure 9.1

You will need to click on the "Cartoon" tab to switch to the "Photo to Cartoon" window. Once you select the online version, all you need to do is load your photo and it converts it to a cartoon – you can change the detail of the cartoon created, but that's the only option available with the online version. To save the newly created toon, you have to capture the screen.

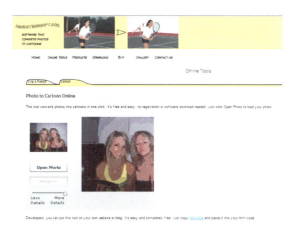

Figure 9.2

The downloaded version has many more options available to use, but remember it is limited to ten conversions. With the downloaded version once it's converted you can either print it or save it. This is really a neat piece of software.

You need to try this one!! Wicked Cool!

38. Comeeko

Cartoons can be used for so many different things. Comeeko at **http://www.comeeko.com/** lets you upload a picture and use that in your comic strip. You can upload a picture of a person or a background and add existing pictures that are provided by Comeeko. Either way this is an interesting comic strip – or as Comeeko calls it a photo strip - creator.

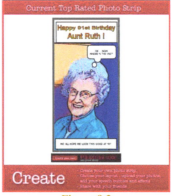

Figure 9.3

As with most of the applications, you will need to create an account to get started. It's easy and it's free. Once you have created your account click on the "Create" tab at the top of the page. The first step is to select the layout for your Photo strip.

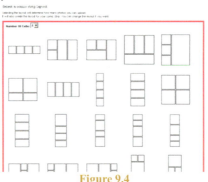

Figure 9.4

You can have up to nine cells in your photo strip with various arrangements as can be seen in Figure 9.4. The layout you select will also determine the number of pictures you can upload. You can change the layout later if you want. At the bottom of the screen is the navigation to the next step. As you can see from Figure 9.5 there are 4 steps to creating your photo strip. Step 1 being select a layout.

You are Here

Figure 9.5

After clicking on "Step 2 Adjust layout" you are directed to a window which will let you manipulate various things that have to do with the cells that will be making up your photo strip, Figure 9.6.

Figure 9.6

You can adjust the border width and color. You can adjust the spacing between the cells and the cell background color. And lastly you can change the color of the photo strip background and the size of the cells. We had some trouble changing these items, We found it easier to just go on to step 3, then come back and adjust these settings. Click on the "Continue to Step 3" where you will create your photo strip. You should get a popup window which explains the creation process.

As seen in Figure 9.7 the actual creation is a four step process.

1. Upload a file from your computer (you can also load a picture from Flickr).
2. Position your file within the cell.
3. Add your speech bubbles and effects.
4. Complete all your other cells.

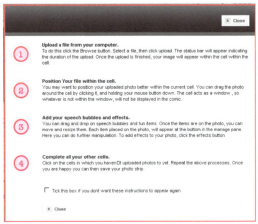

Figure 9.7

As seen in Figure 9.8 there are three areas, the left side are speech bubbles you can add to your cartoon, the right side are effects in the form of images that you can add to your cartoon. You will find a lot of different categories that you can choose from and in the middle is where you begin. Start by doing a browse for an image to upload to your photo strip. If you click on the search tab you can also get and image from Flickr; once uploaded your picture will appear in the first cell of your photo strip. You will need to upload an image for each of your cells in your comic strip. At any time you can preview your comic strip by scrolling down to the panel properties, Figure 9.9.

Figure 9.8

Panel Properties

Figure 9.9

When we clicked on Preview we were able to see how our comic strip was turning out, Figure 9.10.

Figure 9.10

The panel properties window will also let you change any of the items you have added to your cell. Just click on effects next to the item you want to change.

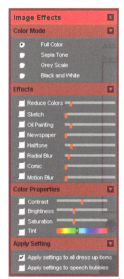

Figure 9.11

Figure 9.11 shows all the affects you have control over for the image we used in our cell.

When you are done creating your comic strip click on the Save button in the panel properties box; your screen will look like Figure 9.12.

Figure 9.12

Then click on the "Save" icon. This will upload it to the Comeeko web site.

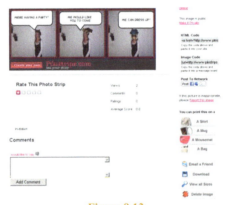

Figure 9.13

Click on the "make it private" button to make your comic strip private. Then click on "Download" to save the comic strip to your hard drive. It will save it as a jpeg file. You can down insert it into any application that will let you place an image. You can keep your comic strip on the Comeeko web site so you can make changes to it later or delete it. This is Wicked Cool.

39. Myths And Legends

Myths and Legends at **http://myths.e2bn.org/** is a fantastic source for creating some really interesting and exciting stories complete with characters, scenery, text and sound. The site itself is built around the idea of creating stories that have been passed on from generation to generation, or just to tell a story - it does not actually need to be old.

Figure 9.14

When you first get to the site take a quick look around. The "Home" tab will give you a quick welcome to Myths and Legends. The "About" tab will give you some information of the whole idea behind the Myths and Legend concept. You can also find links to informational pages, technical requirements, how to use this site, why were the stories told and contact information. The "Myths and Legends" tab will take you to a page where you can see existing stories that have been created by other users. You will find some really great stories that you can look at and listen to. The "Teacher" tab will take you to the teacher's resources. You can even register your school here if you so desire. Actually the Myths and Legends site says it best.

"The variety of stories in Myths and Legends aims to give inspiration to young people at school and at home to create and publish their own work. The site provides a multitude of tools and opportunities that enable pupils to submit their stories for the enjoyment of a worldwide audience, with the prospect of receiving peer review and evaluation."

When we first looked at this web site, what struck us was that we could create our own story. We were not interested in actually creating an existing story, but a way to do a lecture, and make it entertaining. You might say we were getting tired of using the same old PowerPoint slide lectures. So let's see what the "Create your own" tab has to offer. After clicking on the "Create your own tab" you will see Figure 9.15.

Figure 9.15

Wicked Cool Web Stuff 2

As you can see, there are a few ways that you can create a story. You can create a sound or video story if you have a web cam and microphone. You can also upload a story that you have already created.

The option that is most interesting is "Story Creator 2". When you click on the "Story Creator 2" picture you will see Figure 9.16.

Figure 9.16

At first look you might think it is difficult to use, but as it turns out it is pretty easy. The items on the right are the different characters, backgrounds, props and text balloons you can use. You can even upload your own picture to use if you so desire. All the images can be scaled, rotated and placed behind or in front of one another.

At the bottom of the screen you see the "Storyboard" and "Help" buttons. The "Storyboard" button will let you see all the frames in each chapter of your story, Figure 9.17.

Figure 9.17

At the top you see the "Chapter" tabs; your story can have up to ten chapters and each chapter can have up to nine frames. So as you see you can make a good sized story.

So let's create a story. Not just any story, but a lecture that can be used in the classroom. What we were looking for was a way to do a review for an upcoming exam. To give you some of the setting, Halloween was coming up. So here is the first frame that we created, Figure 9.18.

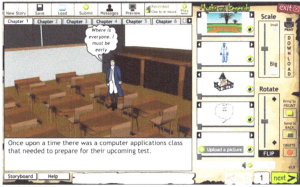

Figure 9.18

It is a little different because you are telling or scripting the story "Once upon a time there was a computer applications class that needed to prepare for their upcoming test" at the same time being able to "cartoon" the story. To place the objects in the frame, just locate the one you want and click on it. You can drag, resize and rotate to position things exactly where you want. Clicking on the "next>" tab will select the next frame. Here's what we created for our second frame.

Figure 9.19

So as you can see the frames are really easy to create – here are the rest of our slides so you can see our complete review, Figure 9.20.

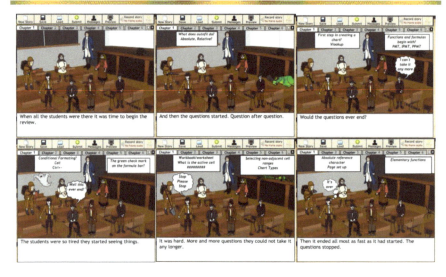

Figure 9.20

When you're done you can preview your story by selecting the "Preview" tab at the top of the screen. When your story is being viewed the script is on the left side instead of at the bottom, Figure 9.21.

Figure 9.21

To save your story, click on the "Save" tab at the top of the screen. This is where you will also be prompted to create an account with Myths and Legends. Go ahead and set up an account – it's free.

What's really great about this site is that you can actually download your story to your computer. By selecting the "download" tab on the right side of the screen, Figure 9.22.

Figure 9.22

You can save your story as a zip file, which you can unzip and play using any browser. You can also print it off and hand it out to a class.

Since we first started using this web site we have created several reviews and lectures. It is a great way to create a lecture that is a lot more enjoyable then watching yet another PowerPoint. You can also record / narrate your script for each frame. What you can do with it in the classroom is only limited by your imagination. Take a look at it - you will love this cartoon story generator. It's Wicked Cool.

40. Blabberize

Very simple, but absolutely a must for using cartoons in the classroom is Blabberize at **http://balbberize.com**. This is such a simple idea; take a picture, animate the mouth of the picture and add your voice. Basically, the mouth moves according to what you say, so it appears as if the figure is talking using your voice. We laugh every time we see this. We have used this many times in both on-line and face-to-face classes.

Figure 9.23

This is the easiest web site to use. You have three choices to select from. If you want to browse, and view other blabberize videos simply click on the "Browse" tab, Figure 9.24.

Figure 9.24

There are some really funny and interesting blabberizings to browse through. It will also give you a really good idea of how others have been using this.

If you click on "My Stuff" you will be prompted to either create an account if you don't have one or log in if you already have an account, Figure 9.25.

Figure 9.25

If you do not have an account, go ahead and create one. With an account you will be able to save your blabberize creations. Did we mention it's free? After you log in you can see your previously created blabberizings. You can actually go back and edit them or delete them. You can also mark them as private which is what we do with the ones we make, Figure 9.26.

Figure 9.26

Ok, so let's get on with how we create a blabberize. As we said it is absolutely simple. When you click on the "Make" tab you will get to the screen asking you to upload an image, Figure 9.27.

Figure 9.27

Just click on the "Browse" to locate an image on your computer. Once you select your image you will have an option to crop the image if you need to. You want to select an image that will show the mouth so that when it is animated it looks good.

Figure 9.28

Once you are happy with your image click on the arrow in the lower right of the screen, Figure 9.28.

Figure 9.29

You're now ready to place the mouth where you want it. Drag it to the mouth on the image, and use the small blue and green dots to size the mouth to fit the image. You can add another mouth if you have a picture with more than one person in it.

Figure 9.30

When we positioned the month for this picture we placed it below the teeth. The part that moves is the part selected, so we didn't want it to look like the teeth moved. The big green dot designates how far the mouth will open, Figure 9.30. You may need to experiment a little but it is really easy to do. When you think you have it the way you want click on the arrow to set up how you are going to supply the voice to your image, Figure 9.31.

Figure 9.31

You can use the microphone on your laptop, upload something you have already recorded and even record using the phone. Yes, we could have her sing a song, by uploading the audio.

Once you have selected how you want to provide the sound you are ready to go. We used the microphone.

Figure 9.32

As we talk the month moves up and down making it seem like the image is talking. It truly never ceases to make us laugh out loud. When you are done recording click on the arrow in the lower right corner, you will then be able to preview and finish your masterpiece.

Figure 9.33

When you are done click on the "OK" button to save it. You can go back to any of the previous options by clicking on the circle on the lower left that takes you to the option that you want to go back to, Figure 9.33.

Figure 9.34

When you click on the "Save" button, Figure 9.34, you will be prompted to title your blabberize, give it a description and add some tags which will help identify it. This is also where you can mark it as private if you so desire, Figure 9.35.

Figure 9.35

Once it is saved you will have several options of how to share it, Figure 9.36.

Figure 9.36

You can copy the URL and send it to whoever you want to be able to see your Blabberize. If you select "Share It!" you will be given the code to embed it as an object on a web page. The "I want this on video" option was not available at the writing of this text, but should be available shortly. When that option becomes available you will be able to save the blabberize as a video to your computer. We can't wait. We have used blabberize many times; here are a few examples of how we have use it in our classes.

We have send out mini lectures. When a student emails us for help on a topic, we have used blabberize to create a short explanation or answer to their question. We have also used it at the beginning of class as a sort of intro to the topic we were talking about. We have placed it on our LMS to thank the students in our class or congratulate them on a job well done. In all cases the students have loved it; as we said it is one of those things that is so simple it just makes you laugh. Wicked Cool!

41. FluxTime

FluxTime at **http://FluxTime.com** is a really interesting animator. After you create your animation you can save to the FluxTime gallery or you can e-mail to someone. If you want a copy of it just e-mail it to yourself.

Figure 9.37

After you click on the "Click here to create a free animation" you will be directed to the FluxTime studio which pops up in its own window, Figure 9.38.

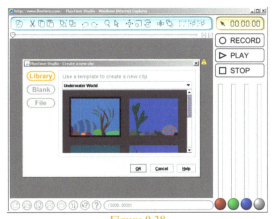

Figure 9.38

It's actually pretty easy to use. You start by selected one of the existing templates. The pull down option on the right side of the "Underwater World" category lets you see the other available categories and templates. There are several categories; Adventures in Space, A Day in the Park and

Christmas Night to mention a few. Once you select your clip, click on ok. We selected Summer on the beach, Figure 9.39.

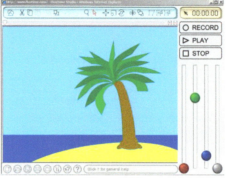

Figure 9.39

The menu bar at the top of the screen has several really neat options. Starting from the left the first icon lets you insert new shapes, text shapes and clips.

Figure 9.40

There is a whole library of clipart to choose from for each of the different categories. You can also select shapes and text or draw your own. The next three icons are your cut, copy and paste features, the two icons following that let you group and ungroup selected shapes. Undo and redo last operations follow next zoom and selection tools after that. Move, scale and rotate are next followed by a flip option to move to back or to front. The last three options let you modify the shapes themselves.

The bottom menu has to do with create, open and save your clips, send and mail when done or post to the gallery.

Last, on the right side of the screen you have record, play and stop, along with color sliders which let you change the color of the selected object. If you play with the tools for a short time you will quickly figure out what they all do.

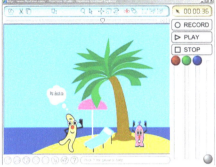

Figure 9.41

To animate your objects select record. Then what ever you do to an object will be recorded, moving rotating, resizing etc. When you are done you can email your creation by clicking on the send and receive button in the bottom menu, Figure 9.42.

Figure 9.42

When you type in the email address you want to send to and who it is coming from the email will look like Figure 9.43.

Figure 9.43

Clicking the link will direct you to the animated ecard.

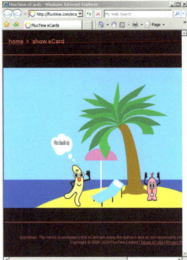

Figure 9.44

We have used this as a way to send a special animation to a student, just letting them know they did a great job in class. Remember it is free. Wicked Cool!

42. Scratch

Here is an actual programming language just for creating comic strips. Get a copy of Scratch at **http://scratch.com** by clicking on the "Download Scratch" link, Figure 9.45.

Figure 9.45

When you start the download process, a form will appear for you to fill out. It's optional, but if you want updates and such it's a great idea. If you don't want to fill it in, just click on the "continue to scratch download" button at the bottom of the form, Figure 9.46.

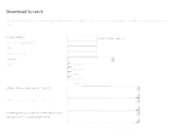

Figure 9.46

If you fill the form in or not, after clicking on the "Continue to Scratch download" button you will be directed to the download page. Select the operating environment you are using and click on the icon, Figure 9.47.

Figure 9.47

Once you download Scratch and run it you should get to the opening screen, Figure 9.48.

Figure 9.48

This is such a great piece of software. The screen is broken up in to several areas. The area on the right is the stage where you create your cartoon. On the stage is the "sprite". The sprite is what you are going to control. You can change how it looks by giving it a different costume, which is basically another sprite. You can also give an instruction to a sprite to tell it to move, react to something, like another sprite or even play music.

The middle of the screen is the "scripts area". This is where you describe, using building blocks, what you want the sprite to do. On the left, the "blocks palette" are the building blocks that you can use to control your sprite.

Ok so let's see if we can take it for a simple test drive to get the feel for how it works. As you can see there is an initial sprite already there. You can select a different sprite by clicking on the "choose new sprite from file" icon located on the right side-middle folder.

Figure 9.49

As you can see there are a lot of different sprites that you can select from. We should mention you can also create your own sprite either by drawing one or uploading one.

For sake of example let's just do something simple with what we have. Select the "move 10 steps" building block and drag it to the "scripts area" then select the "turn 15 degrees" block and move it to the "scripts area". In the scripts area slide the two blocks together, so they interlock. What you have told your sprite to do is move 10 steps and then turn 15 degrees, Figure 9.50.

Figure 9.50

The next thing is to get your sprite to actually do the task. Click on the "control" tab in the "blocks palette" area, Figure 9.51.

Figure 9.51

These are how you can control what and when your sprite does something. Let's make it easy; click on the "when (green flag) clicked" control and drag to the "script" area. Attach it to the top of the script that you already have. Now if you want to see him move 10 steps and then turn 15 degrees click on the green flag in the stage area. Not real impressive, but you can change the number of steps and you will then see him move a little further. As you can see the steps are pretty small. Let's add another control. Drag the "forever" block over and put it around the "move 10 steps" and "rotate 15 degrees" blocks, Figure 9.52.

Figure 9.52

Now click on the green flag in the script area. Your sprite should be going around in a circle. Pretty cool. So here is one you can try.

Figure 9.53

He just runs across the screen saying "I'm running" and then when he stops he says "I'm so tired". There is a lot of information on the web site to get you up to where you can create some really fun things in no time at all. This is really fun.

Once you are happy with what you have, save your project by clicking on the File-save option, this saves a copy of your project so if you want you can come back and make changes to it later. When you are ready to let everyone else see it click on the "Share" option, you will need to create an account with "Stretch", but it is free so no worries, basically they will want a username and password along with some other information. Once your account is created you can upload your creation to their web site, figure 9.54.

Figure 9.54

Once uploaded, click on the title, in this case "Sample", this will take you to the animated cartoon and a place where you can get the code to embed your cartoon or a URL you can send your students to view it, Figure 9.55.

Figure 9.55

Click on the "Embed" link to get to the code and Url. We really like this. As stated on the Scratch web site "Scratch is a new programming language that makes it easy to create your own interactive stories, animations, games, music, and art -- and share your creations on the web.Scratch is designed to help young people (ages 8 and up) develop 21st century learning skills. As they create and share Scratch projects, young people learn important mathematical and computational ideas, while also learning to think creatively, reason systematically, and work collaboratively." This is Wicked Cool.

43. Fuzzwich

Here is a really simple and neat animated cartoon creator. Fuzzwich at **http://www.fuxxwich.com** is by far one of the easier to use Web based animated cartoon creators.

Figure 9.56

There is no log in or registering required to use Fuzzwich. To begin click on the "Make one now" icon, Figure 9.56.

Figure 9.57

It's a simple three step process. As you can see from Figure 9.57 you begin by selecting your background. If you do not see any particular background you like you can upload one of your own. Once you have selected the background you like step two lets you select the character you would like to use in your animated cartoon, Figure 9.58.

Figure 9.58

You can have more than one character - either select them all now, or later when you are creating your cartoon. Once you have selected a character you will be prompted to "just add it" or "customize with your face". This is where Fuzzwich is a little different.

Figure 9.59

If you click on "Just add it" you will be directed back to select another character if you want to, but if you select "Customize with your face" you are given the option to upload a picture and grab the face from it or if you have a web cam you can get a picture from there. Here's what you get after you click on "Customize with your face", Figure 9.60.

Figure 9.60

If you select "Upload" you are prompted to find a picture and upload it. If you select "Webcam", a picture from your web cam shows up on the screen with an option to take a picture. It's pretty cool. Either way you will have a picture with a face on it to work with. We uploaded a photo, Figure 9.61.

Figure 9.61

Wicked Cool Web Stuff 2

Once your photo is uploaded use the green dots to encompass the face portion of the picture. You can create more green dots by clicking on the outline, this way you can trace precisely around the head, Figure 9.62.

Figure 9.62

Here you can see how we have placed the green dots to outline the head area. Don't worry you can shrink the head down to a size that will fit the character you have selected. When you are done Click on the "Next" button.

Figure 9.63

As you can see the head is a little large for the character. The slide bar on the left will let you resize the head. You can also click and drag the head to better position it if you need to. The teeter totter at the bottom will let you rotate the head if that looks better.

Figure 9.64

As you can see it's easy to do. After you are finished click on the "Done!" button to return to the list of characters, Figure 9.65.

Figure 9.65

If you want you can select another character or you can wait and select one later. After you are finished selecting your characters click on the "Done!" button to continue.

Figure 9.66

So now you are ready to create your animated cartoon. The animation is limited to 20 seconds so you might want to plan ahead. It's pretty simple to do. The "REC" feature is to record the movement of the characters. You move the characters by dragging them. There is a "Plus sign" in the upper left of the screen which will let you add more characters. You can also add a music background song by clicking on the "music sign" on the lower right of the screen. So for example we positioned our character on the left side of the screen and then got another character by clicking on the "plus sign", Figure 9.67.

Figure 9.67

You will notice when you click on a character you can apply an action or a speech bubble, but more about that in a minute. Start the recorder and move your characters. You will see the recorder slide move. You can pause your recording at any time to add an action or speech bubble or you can do all your movements first and add your actions and speech bubbles at the end. You can also position the recorder slider to re-record over part of your recording. As you record and do actions and speech bubbles, you will see where they are occurring by the icon placed on the recorder slide.

Figure 9.68

You can preview at any time by clicking on the preview button at the top right of the screen, Figure 9.69.

Figure 9.69

Wicked Cool Web Stuff 2

After you are done with your "minivid" click on the "check mark" in the upper right of the screen. You will be asked to give your animated cartoon a name and say who created it. When you type in who created it, we would suggest you type "by *and then your name*", something like "by Beebe". Once you click on the "check mark" you will be given the URL or Object code that you can embed in a web page. The biggest problem with Fuzzwich is that once it is created you cannot go back and edit it. It is also public with no way to make it private. On the other hand there is no login or registration to create it. So here are the highlights of our animated cartoon created with Fuzzwich.

Figure 9.70

We have used this several times. The 20 second limit on the size of the video was a problem for us at first, but with a little practice it seems like it is definitely long enough to say what you want to say. So Wicked Cool.

44. Voki

Have you ever wanted to create your own personalized speaking avatar? Just think of the possibilities. You could create a message to a friend and have your avatar say it. Voki at **http://www.voki.com/** is such a service and it's free.

Figure 9.71

The Web page gives a lot of great ideas how you might use this tool. You will need to create an account by supplying your e-mail address and a password, but again remember it is free and they do not spam you. To begin, click on the "create" tab.

Figure 9.72

To create your avatar, start by selecting a character. Select the Left most icon under the "Customize Your Character" text.

Figure 9.73

You will have a lot of characters to select from as you can see from Figure 9.73. The characters can also be characterized by type and male or female. So take a look around and select one that you really like. We selected the bear in the "animals" category, Figure 9.74.

Figure 9.74

Right underneath the Avatar you can change the size of the mouth, nose, body, height and width. You can also click on the "Color" tab to change the colors of the bear if you so choose. For whatever character you choose you can change the clothing and add bling by clicking on the clothing and bling tabs. We gave our avatar a different shirt and hat and for bling a pair of sun glasses.

Figure 9.75

After you are done making changes to your avatar click on the "Done" tab at the bottom of the "Customize You Character" window. You can now change the background and player.

Figure 9.76

Wicked Cool Web Stuff 2

For backgrounds we selected indoor and a bedroom, since our Voki is in a nightshirt. The player is what surrounds your avatar. We selected a green player, Figure 9.77.

Figure 9.77

So the only thing left is to add something for our avatar to say. Basically "Give It A Voice". There are several ways you can give your avatar a voice. You can type your text, which is what we use most often; you can also record your message by phone. We think this is really cool. You give your phone number and shortly you receive a phone call. Just say what you want your avatar to say and hang up. The neat thing about this is the avatar speaks in your voice. If you have a microphone attached to your computer or a built in microphone you can also record your message and still have your avatar speak in your voice. If you have a prerecorded sound file you can upload it and use it for the voice of your Voki. We think all the bases have been covered for giving your Voki a voice. Try each one, you will be amazed at how easy it is to use.

When you are done click on the "Publish" tab at the bottom of the screen, Figure 9.78.

Figure 9.78

You will be asked to supply a title for your newly created Voki.

Figure 9.79

Type in a title and click the "Save" tab. After a few moments you will be presented with ways to use your newly created Voki.

Figure 9.80

We have used this many times. One of the things that has been added by the Voki team is "Voki for Education". By clicking on the link you can find various ways that Vokis are being used in education. Summing it all up:

- Create speaking avatars/characters
- Personalized avatars (animal, cartoon, human)
- Personalized voice and accent (via phone, microphone, text to speech or upload file)
- No more than a minute.
- Personalized background
- Can be shared through email or posted in wikis, blogs or websites.

This is a really cool - we mean a Wicked Cool web site.

Chapter 10 – Discovery

Discovery is such a wonderful name for a chapter. In this category we placed those web applications that discover things or solve a problem. WolframAlpha is what is called a computational knowledge engine. You can ask a question and it will search through its knowledge base and give you an answer. Project Gutenberg is a whole library of e-books that you can read for free. What a great web site and application. Birth lets you view events for a particular year. Just type in the year and the screen will continuously show events that occurred during that time. We also included Addict-o-matic which will search through social media looking for information about a name you type in. It will give you all the places where that name appears.

45. WolframAlpha

Have you ever wanted to figure out the answer to a Math problem – well not just the answer, but how you got the answer, showing all the steps along the way? What you need is a computational knowledge engine. Take a look at Wolfram/Alpha computational knowledge engine at **http://wolframalpha.com** Figure 10.1.

All you do is pose a question or calculation and Wolfram Alpha formulates an answer by using the expert knowledge in its databases. This is really fantastic. I typed in (5.3/3)*22+5

Figure 10.2

It gave us an immediate answer as we were typing it in, but then when we hit the enter key, it expanded to give us how the problem was done, Figure 10.3.

Figure 10.3

Mathematics is just one of the things it has knowledge about; actually you can pose questions about many different areas. Physics, chemistry, education and life science are just a few. Figure 10.4 shows what we discovered when we typed in "Blue".

Figure 10.4

When we typed in Microsoft it gave us a wealth of information. Actually any word we typed in it came back and gave a wealth of information.

This is something that everyone should learn about and use; it's Wicked Cool!

46. Project Gutenberg

 This has got to be a must for everyone who wants to read e-books. Project Gutenberg at **http://www.gutenberg.org** is the oldest and largest producer of free and public domain e-books (electronic books).

Figure 10.5

"**Project Gutenberg** offers over 36,000 free e-books to download to your PC, Kindle, iPad, iPhone, Android or other portable device. Choose between ePub, Kindle, HTML and simple text formats.

We carry high quality ebooks: All our ebooks were previously published by *bona fide* publishers. We digitized and diligently proofed them with the help of thousands of volunteers.

No fee or registration is required, but if you find Project Gutenberg useful, we kindly ask you to donate a small amount so we can buy and digitize more books. Other ways to help include; digitizing more books, recording audio books, or reporting errors.

Over 100,000 free ebooks are available through our Partners, Affiliates and Resources. "

Figure 10.6 shows the screen after you click on "Catalog". The catalog will let you search for books by title or author.

Figure 10.6

We have been using this web site for the last few years and it is absolutely great. i.e. Wicked Cool!

47. Birth

This is pretty interesting; check out what happened in your birth year at **www.whathappenedinmybirthyear.com**, Figure 10.7.

Figure 10.7

Just type in a year and the show begins – I typed in 1963 (not really my birth year).

You will see it count down from the current year to 1963 and then it will start listing events from 1963, Figure 10.8.

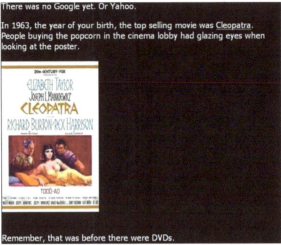

There was no Google yet. Or Yahoo.

In 1963, the year of your birth, the top selling movie was Cleopatra. People buying the popcorn in the cinema lobby had glazing eyes when looking at the poster.

Remember, that was before there were DVDs.

Figure 10.8

It goes on and on, I'm not sure for how long, but it is really interesting and Wicked Cool!

48. Addictomatic

Have you ever wanted to browse all the social media sites looking for information about a particular topic? Maybe your name or a friend's name. Addictomatic at **http://addictomatic.com/** will let you do just that, Figure 10.9.

Figure 10.9

Just type in a topic and it searches through all the different media looking for things that pertain to the topic. After trying to think of someones name to look up we decided on our son. Figure 10.10 gives a rundown of what Addictomatic came back with. As you can see it's pretty interesting.

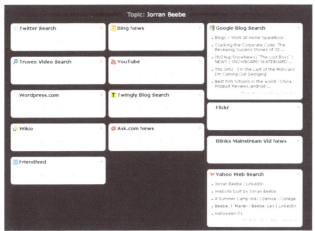

Figure 10.10

If you move your cursor over any of the links it will give your more information.

Figure 10.11 shows what we got after we typed in Obama.

Figure 10.11

You can see it checks out pretty much all media looking for anything in relation to the topic.

This is an interesting and Wicked Cool site.

Chapter 11 – Mailing and Markups

We have all used email, at least we think so, but even email is changing. Wouldn't it be cool if you could make a video email and send it? Eyejot does exactly that. Ccreate a video of yourself using your web cam and then email to any valid email address. Crocodoc will let you view and comment on any document. Both these applications are Wicked Cool.

49. Eyejot

Have you ever wanted to send a video email? Create a video of yourself talking and then send it? No more typing, no more spell check, and a heck of a lot more fun. Eyejot at **http://www.eyejot.com/** will let you do exactly that, Figure 11.1.

Figure 11.1

You will need a video camera to use this, but it's worth the investment if you don't already have one.

"Eyejot is the first, comprehensive, client-free online video messaging platform ideal for both personal and business communications. It offers everyone the ability to create and receive video messages in a self-contained, spam-free environment. With no client to install, you can start using Eyejot immediately with any browser, on any platform. It even features built-in support for iTunes™ (and iPods&trade), mobile devices and social networks like MySpace™."

To start, set up an account by clicking on the "Join now for free" button. Once you have an account you can log in and start sending video email.

Figure 11.2

Just click on the "Compose new Message" button to begin. Once your message/video is created, you can email to anyone with a valid e-mail address. You have all the capabilities of an email package; the difference is you are sending video emails. Wicked Cool!

50. Crocodoc

"View & Comment on Any Document". Crocodoc at **http://crocodoc.com** is a free application which will let you upload your document, annotate it and then download it with annotations as a PDF file.

Figure 11.3

This is a great tool for when you want to comment on a document. Click on the "Upload Document" button.

Figure 11.4

We uploaded an image; once it's uploaded you can add a comment to it, draw, and add text, highlight and strikeout. Pretty much all the tools you need to mark up a paper, Figure 11.5.

Figure 11.5

When you're done click on the download option on the right side, Figure 11.6.

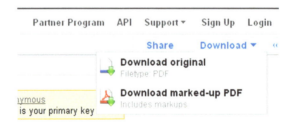

Figure 11.6

You can download the original or the original with the added markups. This has been a real time saver in trying to explain things. Definitely Wicked Cool!

Appendix A

19. Tagxedo
    - http://www.tagxedo.com/
20. Typemirror
    - http://typemirror.com/
21. Phonespell
    - http://www.phonespell.org
22. Text-Image
    - http://www.text-image.com
23. Star Wars
    - http://asciimation.co.nz/
24. Alice
    - http://www.pandorabots.com/pandora/talk?botid=f5d922d97e345aa1
25. Warning Sign Generator
    - http://www.warningsigngenerator.com/
26. Prison Name Generator
    - http://www.prisonbitchname.com/
27. Voxopop
    - http://www.voxopop.com/
28. Glogster
    - http:// www.glogster.com
29. Wall Wisher
    - http://www.wallwisher.com
30. Bibme
    - http://bibme.org
31. Howjsay
    - http://howjsay.com/
32. Zamzar
    - http://www.zamzar.com/
33. Downforeveryoneorjustme
    - http://www.downforeveryoneorjustme.com/
34. Wakerupper
    - http://wakerupper.com/
35. Monkey on your back
    - http://monkeyon.com
36. Freephnoetracer
    - http://www.freephonetracer.com/
37. Caricaturesoft
    - http://www.caricaturesoft.com/

38. Comeeko
    - http://www.comeeko.com/
39. Myths and Legends
    - http://myths.e2bn.org/
40. Balbberize
    - http://balbberize.com
41. FluxTime
    - http://FluxTime.com
42. Scratch
    - http://scratch.com
43. Fuzzwich
    - http://www.fuxxwich.com
44. Voki
    - http://www.voki.com/
45. Wolframalpha
    - http://www.wolframalpha.com/
46. Project Gutenberg
    - http://www.gutenberg.org
47. Birth
    - www.whathappenedinmybirthyear.com
48. Addictomatic
    - http://addictomatic.com/
49. Eyejot
    - http://www.eyejot.com/
50. Crocodoc
    - http://crocodoc.com

www.ingramcontent.com/pod-product-compliance
Lightning Source LLC
Chambersburg PA
CBHW041141050326
40689CB00001B/443